Commitment to
Higher Education

Titles recently published under the SRHE/Open University Press imprint:

Michael Allen: *The Goals of Universities*
Sir Christopher Ball and Heather Eggins: *Higher Education into the 1990s*
Ronald Barnett: *The Idea of Higher Education*
Tony Becher: *Academic Tribes and Territories*
William Birch: *The Challenge to Higher Education*
David Boud *et al.*: *Teaching in Laboratories*
Heather Eggins: *Restructuring Higher Education*
Colin Evans: *Language People*
Oliver Fulton: *Access and Institutional Change*
Derek Gardiner: *The Anatomy of Supervision*
Gunnar Handal and Per Lauvås: *Promoting Reflective Teaching*
Vivien Hodgson *et al.*: *Beyond Distance Teaching, Towards Open Learning*
Margaret Kinnell: *The Learning Experiences of Overseas Students*
Peter Linklater: *Education and the World of Work*
Graeme Moodie: *Standards and Criteria in Higher Education*
John Pratt and Suzanne Silverman: *Responding to Constraint*
John Radford and David Rose: *A Liberal Science*
Marjorie Reeves: *The Crisis in Higher Education*
John T. E. Richardson *et al.*: *Student Learning*
Derek Robbins: *The Rise of Independent Study*
Geoffrey Squires: *First Degree*
Gordon Taylor *et al.*: *Literacy by Degrees*
Kim Thomas: *Gender and Subject in Higher Education*
Malcolm Tight: *Academic Freedom and Responsibility*
Susan Warner Weil and Ian McGill: *Making Sense of Experiential Learning*
David Watson: *Managing the Modular Course*
Alan Woodley *et al.*: *Choosing to Learn*
John Wyatt: *Commitment to Higher Education*

Commitment to Higher Education

Seven West European Thinkers on the
Essence of the University:
Max Horkheimer, Karl Jaspers,
F. R. Leavis, J. H. Newman,
José Ortega y Gasset, Paul Tillich,
Miguel de Unamuno

John Wyatt

The Society for Research into Higher Education
& Open University Press

To Marjorie

Published by SRHE and
Open University Press
Celtic Court
22 Ballmoor
Buckingham MX18 1XW

and

1900 Frost Road, Suite 101
Bristol, PA 19007, USA

First Published 1990

British Library Cataloguing in Publication Data

Commitment to Higher Education: Seven West European
    thinkers on the essence of the University.
    1. Society. Role of Universities
    I. Horkheimer, Max   II. Wyatt, John
    378'.103

    ISBN 0-335-09371-X

Library of Congress Cataloging-in-Publication Data

Commitment to Higher Education: seven West European thinkers on the
    essence of the university/Max Horkheimer . . . [et al.]: John Wyatt
    [editor].
        p. cm.
    ISBN 0-335-09371-X
    1. Education, Higher—Europe—Philosophy. I. Horkheimer, Max,
    1895–1973.   II. Wyatt, John, 1931–
    LA628.C54   1990
    378.4—dc20   89-48478 CIP

Typeset by Rowland Phototypesetting Limited,
Bury St Edmunds, Suffolk
Printed in Great Britain by St Edmundsbury Press Limited,
Bury St Edmunds, Suffolk

Contents

Acknowledgements

The origins of this book lie partly in the author's own experience of higher education, but mainly in the dialogue which he has been privileged to share. The obvious 'dialogue' has been with the books and papers detailed in the ensuing chapters, but the true dialogue has been with colleagues and fellow enquirers into the nature of educational institutions. Pre-eminent among these have been my colleague-trustees of the Higher Education Foundation. They and the members of the Higher Education Group at the annual conference have sometimes unnerved and sent me back to think again, but always inspired. I am not alone in being deeply in debt to the distinguished President of the Higher Education Foundation, Professor Roy Niblett, who has been a wise and stimulating guide to me personally. This book arises from his direct and shrewd encouragement. Among colleagues of the West Sussex Institute, I want to thank Dr Keith Jenkins for many suggestions about the protagonists in the history of ideas, Dr Bill Gray who collaborated with me on an article on Horkheimer and without whose translation of the Horkheimer inaugural address nothing could have been achieved, and Robert Hamlin, some-time Principal Librarian of the Institute, who used his Spanish (with courage) to help me to interpret the two rectoral addresses of Unamuno. All the people mentioned above have been invaluable. They are not to blame for any failings or errors in the ensuing pages.

The chapter on Horkheimer is a rewritten version of a joint article (with Bill Gray) appearing in *The Journal of Applied Philosophy* (Vol. 2, No. 1, 1985). *Studies in Higher Education* (Vol. 6, No. 1, 1981 and Vol. 7, No. 1, 1982) published articles by me on Ortega y Gasset and Karl Jaspers, which were rewritten for the two chapters on these thinkers. I first discussed Paul Tillich and Miguel de Unamuno in a shorter form in the *Higher Education Newsletter* (now called *Reflections*). I am very grateful to the editors of these journals for their ready agreement to re-use and change material that first appeared in, and was encouraged by, their publications.

Extracts are reprinted from *From The Intellectual Legacy of Paul Tillich* (1969) by J. Lyons by permission of the Wayne State University Press.

Finally, but far from least, I want to thank the typists who have worked so cheerfully on the drafts of this book. I am very grateful indeed for the interest and care they always take with work of this kind. They have chiefly been Debbie

Bates, Gill Brady and Isabel Cherrett. They are a vital part of an academic community, which, ultimately, has been the foremost impulse and inspiration to seek guidance from the great minds of the past.

1

Introduction: Voices to be Heard

The purpose of this book is to bring back to public attention seven thinkers who wrote about what they believed to be vital in higher education. I hope its audience will be those who are concerned about higher education in Western Europe. The argument they will find here is that the voices of these seven thinkers should play their part in the current public debates about higher education. This statement implies that these writers are not, at present, heard. Apart from the first one to be considered, J. H. Newman, it is broadly true that their writings on education are ignored, and I shall attempt to say why this is the case. Before doing so, there are two important preliminaries to be made. The first is that, partly for convenience, and partly because six of the seven writers restricted themselves to the word, 'university' is used throughout to mean university, polytechnic, college or institute, or any other designation that is individually used, rather than the much more clumsy phrase 'institution of higher education'. It is perhaps a mark of our contemporary difficulties, as well as a measure of the relatively recent growth of higher education, that, without an explanation, one word will not do.

The second preliminary comment is also one of terminology. The activity this book engages in (because the writers analysed in the book themselves engage in it), I call 'philosophy of higher education'. With such a well-worn and well-masticated word like 'philosophy', it is often easier to state what it is not, rather than what it is. This is not a text for the linguistic analysis of questions about the nature of knowledge, although all the writers use the word 'knowledge' with frequency and ease. Epistemological questions about 'what it means to ask this question' are not in this field of discourse. The main attention of these writers is about how and why people in universities learn, as much as about what they learn. Some were as fully aware as their contemporaries about analytical enquiries into 'How do I know?' and 'How do I know I am knowing?', but their main thrust is much more ancient and therefore criticized by professional colleagues for being so. They are more likely to use words like 'the pursuit of Truth' or 'the culture of the intellect' or 'the vital system of ideas'. Such a way of going on excluded them from the camp of professional philosophy for a long time and, as I shall say later, is one reason for their disappearance from public debates. The word 'philosophy' which I use here and share with the writers is much closer to Brubacher's use of the term in the title of his American study *On the Philosophy of Higher Education* (Brubacher 1982). In that important text, which has no comparable example in Western Europe, he sets out his aim in layman's terms: 'to clarify the problem and balance its pros and cons by more fundamental considerations' (Brubacher 1982: 5).

The seven writers here are indeed concerned with fundamental considerations; they are all deep diggers. More than digging deep, they also believe there is something to look for. Their understanding of 'philosophy' is therefore about meaning. This they share with contemporary linguistically oriented philosophers. However, they are seeking further, and with more zest in the other sense of meaning – the meaning of the experience of learning to the tutor and to the student, the meaning of the university to the general purposes of the state, and so on. They are writing about Aristotelian 'formal causes' or why an institution exists. They also propose solutions as well as analyse problems. If a common title must be found to bring all their works together, it would have to be *The Idea of a University*, the very title selected by two of them, Newman and Jaspers. Each has an idea, in two senses: the sense of an 'ideal' of a place of learning and the older sense of 'the essential end' or objective. Once again, this language defines the kind of philosophers presented here.

The first writer is selected because he represents almost an archetype of the committed intellectual who proposes what a university should be. It is, of course, John Henry Newman (1801–1890), and the main text is the influential *The Idea of a University*. Why a text of 1852, first delivered to inaugurate a new Catholic university, by its new rector who was not to keep the post for very long, should have such a long-lasting influence all over the world may be answered by the second chapter of this book. It would certainly be answered by time spent on the major text itself, which is very accessible. Although there are world-famous works within each of the other writers' list of publications, the educational texts, and specifically their notions of a university, are much less well known, even by title. In some cases, the text put forward here as a 'key text' has not been analysed in English before. The 'key texts' were first written or presented as addresses within a period of some 17 years, between 1930 and 1947, in times of European crisis and war. Hannah Arendt's phrase, 'Men of Dark Times', would apply to all of them. Before turning to the 'key texts' and the method of analysing them and related writings, I shall briefly introduce the actors who are to play their roles in the following chapters.

José Ortega y Gasset (1883–1955) is presented as the first of the twentieth-century writers after Newman, because he illustrates a somewhat simple and straightforward, but nevertheless passionately convinced argument for a public role for the university. His concentration is focused on the notion of culture, through a restricted curriculum, or 'doctrine of parsimony' as I shall call it. It is a good reminder of the close connection between what is to be studied as well as the public role of the university. Ortega presented *Mission of the University*, when he held a chair in the University of Madrid in 1930.

Karl Jaspers (1883–1969) follows, and this chapter is one of the longest for the simple reason that he presents a grand design with considerable elaboration of many of the main themes of other writers. Jaspers also turns our attention to curricular matters, but in a very different manner, integrated with his understanding of human knowledge and with an emphasis on the vital issue of communication in a university. His prophetic interpretation of 'boundary situations' is unique but should leave echoes to be picked up in subsequent chapters with other writers. The text, *The Idea of the University*, was first issued in the 1920s, but the enlarged version, later available in English, was published in 1947 when Jaspers was reinstated to his chair in the University of Heidelberg.

Max Horkheimer (1895–1973) is placed after Jaspers partly because they worked under the same grim shadows of the 1930s in Germany, but also because he too was working on the issue of interdisciplinary studies, within the more confined context of the Frankfurt Institute for Social Research. The 'key text' is an address given when he became Director of the Frankfurt Institute for Social Research in 1931.

Frank Richard Leavis (1895–1978) (or F. R. Leavis as he is much more usually known) is included immediately after Horkheimer because he too, in a very different way, proposes one subject area as a humane centre of the university. As with all these brief introductions, great damage is done by introducing one single issue from their work. A much wider and richer range of thinking emerges in this instance as in others. The origin of the chief work that engages attention here was a series of articles in the journal *Scrutiny*, published in the early 1930s, eventually producing a book in 1943.

The two final writers are similarly well known in their own fields, but not directly for work in education. They are Paul Tillich (1886–1965) and Miguel de Unamuno (1864–1934). Tillich's comments on higher education are scattered in a range of works, but he aptly demonstrates the 'culture of intellect', through his own experiences of life in universities, which Newman, Ortega and Leavis had developed. Unamuno's key texts are two addresses as rector of the University of Salamanca given in very dark times indeed at the onset of the Spanish Civil War. Unamuno is chosen to end this series, despite being the oldest of the twentieth-century writers, because he leaves a message of hope for the enquiring, 'curious' mind. He also attempts to define a major public role for the university.

The 'key texts' and the common pursuit

In the history of ideas there is no shortage of raw materials or prime sources for study. People who live by ideas share them almost by definition. They write or have their speeches recorded by others and in their turn are talked about and written about. Ideas about ideas might readily be called 'The Great Debate', and never more so than when the subject is the very environment where ideas are supposed to have their most appropriate habitat, the university. So we are not short of texts to analyse, of speeches to put under detailed scrutiny, or of public records of opinions about the house of intellect. The word 'debate', however, almost presumes a stability and an orderly period of peace, if not within the hearts of the participants, at least in the security of the arena of debate. You can argue 'ambulando', but hardly on the run. In times of crisis when the very security of the institution seems to be threatened, the calmness of pro and contra argument appears to be a luxury. Arguments for defence and prosecution are more likely than proposals and speeches of opposition in a debating chamber. Such is the present time in Western Europe and the USA. One thinks of the passionate argument for the return of true philosophy as a contributor to the discussion about the corroded university made by Allan Bloom (1987: 312) in *The Closing of the American Mind*:

> Our present educational problems cannot seriously be attributed to bad administration, weakness of will, lack of discipline, lack of money, insufficient attention to the three R's, or any of the other common explanations that indicate things will be set right if we professors would just 'pull up our socks'. All these things are the result of a deeper lack of belief in the university's vocation.

If it is true that the debate has degenerated into pleas for survival, where can we look amidst the mass of written evidence available for a deeper discussion to remind those inside and outside higher education why they should begin to believe in themselves and their institutions again?

There are, of course, certain classical sources, such as public documents, most often from commissions or committees. They, and other weighty bundles of evidence, proliferate at moments of political decision. One thinks of the massive commissions of Victorian times on Oxford and Cambridge, or the Robbins Report of 1963 in the UK, the nineteenth-century Yale Faculty Report and the 1970s Carnegie Commission Reports in the USA. They prove to be very valuable sources for those pursuing the history of ideas, often revealing more about those giving evidence and about implicit beliefs and values than about the constitutions they proposed and the structures they rejected. A different scale of sources, but equally revealing, is found when those actively engaged in the academic profession make oracular statements at crucial moments highly charged with threatening decisions, but also at calmer moments such as a time of academic ritual. These documents, inaugural lectures, specially prepared texts or specially written personal pleas in threatening times, can be powerful signals not only for the contemporary protagonists but also for the future. Senior members of the academic society who deliver this kind of statement are predisposed to dream as well as to defend the nature of the institution they work for or wish to work for. The *locus classicus* is John Henry Newman's *The Idea of a University*. In a sense, this seminal text was a piece of Utopianism. The university Newman describes did not exist except in his selective memory of the best of Oxford and in his ambitions for a Catholic intellectual kingdom on earth. It was nevertheless of profound importance in establishing the guidelines for debate in the house of intellect for at least a century to follow. Because Newman's *The Idea of a University* has been so seminal, the second chapter of this book is dedicated to it. Although there have been few 'moments' of similar power, there have been some and this study continues by giving an opportunity to 'listen' to six such occasions when statements were made. Some are 'inaugural' occasions, others are books developed from an occasion, one is a brief reminiscence.

The most critical studies about the philosophy of higher education have emanated from the USA, a society frequently committed to open, public debate on social purposes. Western European statements on the same scale appear to be less noticeable. It is partly to set this record straight, at least by concentrating, with the exception of Newman, on one short period of intellectual activity in mid-century, that this account is written. This set of Western European thinkers at a particular point in their own intellectual voyage, delivered firm statements about the nature of the universities or colleges they already led or about the improvements they wished to see. Four of the thinkers (Ortega y Gasset, Max Horkheimer, Karl Jaspers and F. R. Leavis) write documents not unlike Newman's great work, in that they consider the shape of an institution which is due to be reformed or an ideal one which they believe could come to life. The other two (Paul Tillich and Miguel de Unamuno) present texts which are less closely related to instances of the founding of an institution, but have important things to say about what was to them the ideal form of higher education system. What is common to all of them is their professional lives. They were all academics earning their daily bread by teaching, writing and studying in the kind of institutions they aimed to justify or to criticize. All held teaching positions. Three (Unamuno, Jaspers and Horkheimer) held ultimate responsibility as Rector or Director of a university or similar institution. Experience tempers all their thinking.

The Western European tradition

These writers also shared another common feature, their European experience. This book turns attention to Western European writers deliberately because, in the English-speaking academic community particularly, and perhaps elsewhere, there is no shortage of texts on American work (see, e.g. Barzun 1968; Brubacher 1982; Kerr 1963). All are of great value, but there is at the present time a singular neglect of a fruitful period of the intellectual history of ideas with its ferment at its greatest around the mid-point of the century. It is as if a period of intellectual excitement has been declared out-of-date and unfashionable, a charge that will be explored. All the continental writers under consideration shared the 'dark times' of Europe. Ortega and Unamuno had long periods of exile from Spain; Tillich and Horkheimer were forced to find refuge in the USA. Jaspers lived in virtual house arrest, continually at considerable personal risk in Nazi Germany. Both Newman and Leavis, for totally different reasons, had serious estrangements from their Alma Mater. These episodes contributed to the intensity of their writing on such issues as academic freedom, but, as this book hopes to demonstrate, the extremity of their experience never had the effect of diminishing the importance of what again they all share: a doctrine of hope.

Excluding Newman, the writers do not come from any one philosophical tradition, although they form overlapping sets within Western European philosophical movements of the mid-century. 'Existentialism' might include loosely (very loosely) Ortega y Gassett, but with a much better fit for Jaspers and Tillich. 'Vitalism' is discernible in both Unamuno and Ortega. F. R. Leavis is in a mainstream of English liberal thought linking Coleridge and Matthew Arnold, and a form of Marxism (far from orthodox) is undoubtedly a major part of Horkheimer's intellectual position. Rather than straining to categorize the thinkers, I have attempted to let them speak for themselves, with my own commentary on their intellectual home base only when it seemed to be appropriate. Of far more importance is their overall intellectual colour. In general, they all challenged in their own times the pervading consensus of power, both political and academic. As we survey them from the dubious advantage point of our own complicated decades at the end of the century, we can appreciate why their resistance to totalitarian forces was so impassioned. Conversely, these writers also represent an opposition to unthinking liberal idealism. In many ways, it would be true to say that all represent a conservative stance in intellectual matters. I have not found this position to be a contradiction to the claim of the previous paragraph that they are united in optimism. Finally, in relation to 'belongingness', their academic 'trades' varied considerably. They taught sociology, economics, history, literature, metaphysics, politics and theology, but they are united in being broadly, if not narrowly, and from time to time, if not permanently, philosophers.

My personal interest in this group of writers arises from my own day-to-day concern over the last 20 years of managing three institutions of higher education. The institution I currently care for has had to be explicit in arguing for its place in the family of higher education and, week by week, year by year has had to justify staying in that charmed circle. When I turned to the library shelves on higher education for intellectual refreshment and support in the task of founding and reforming an institution, I found much repetition of arguments about contemporary functions (the 'what for' arguments) but little consideration of value (the 'why'). There were volumes of texts on the economic justification of types of institutions, which seemed to correspond neither to the institution I am privileged to lead nor to the universities and colleges of much longer standing with which I have worked for 25 years. Indeed, time spent with contemporary literature can be corrosive of confidence, for, since the 1960s, there has been a body of writing highly critical of institutions in any shape or form. Much of the popular philosophy of education is irredeemably pessimistic about the nature of institutions and of those foolish or power-crazed enough to lead them. Schools, colleges and universities, in the minds of these schools of thought, bear the mark of original sin; they are engines of 'inauthentic being', organizations for the perversion of truth. The writers in this volume, however, by the very nature of their employment and because of their own dramatic professional history, were almost under compulsion to bring forth a philosophy of institutions. They were therefore at risk of being vested deliverers of vested interests, but, precisely when they are at their most personally revealing, they produce an argument of value to fellow practitioners.

Why these writers have been excluded from recent debate

The previous paragraph, and indeed the opening of this introduction, presuppose that not only are there people who have spoken about the idea of the university, but also that there are listeners 'out there' who might hear them and join in the great debate. One of the reasons for writing this book, is to bring back into the arena of argument this group of men so that what they say can be taken up, at least challenged and, at best, contribute to a swell of opinion and ideas about higher education. I still firmly believe 'ideas have legs' and I hope that more ideas, not less, will start to move around. This statement brings to the fore a major difficulty, at least, about the twentieth-century thinkers in this volume (can we safely assume that Newman is permanently discussable?). In presenting this group of thinkers, one frequently meets the response that they are no longer relevant. They are, it is alleged, imprisoned in their own time and so offer no remedies for the afflictions of the end of the century. They are condemned, for instance, for not offering a usable language for a solution to the problems of funding mass higher education. Yet, how could they write about what they had never experienced? For many preoccupied vice chancellors and bursars they could indeed be said to be a different language group, users of a dialect, explaining the university as a phenomenon in a way which might bring an embarrassed chill to senates and committee rooms in the 1980s and 1990s. Indeed, the problem for the commentator on Ortega, Unamuno, Jaspers, Tillich, Horkheimer and Leavis is less one of explication of what they said, and more of a problem of submitting a request for a ticket to be admitted to the currently permitted arena of debate. It is an intriguing question to answer. Why is it that these thinkers are judged to be 'dated' and virtually invisible, when the institutions they write about and wished to have discussed have, in fact, moved more and more into the public gaze?

One of the most obvious ways by which an intellectual circle excludes a way of thought from its field of discussion is to assert that the contestant is 'dated'. No more condemning word in the academic vocabulary could be imagined. This is a particularly twentieth-century slur. The culture of 'the new' and the domination of notions of fashion is remarkably similar to the language of commerce, of production, growth and obsolescence. Ideas are discarded merely because of the date of their first production. The abandonment of previous thinkers goes deeper than the applied economics of 'last year's model', or even beyond a crude belief in progressivism based on the slogan 'What is new is better than what came before'. A more significant modern intellectual objection to listening to these thinkers, including Newman, is a steadily increasing distrust of thinkers of the past because of the implied partiality of their stance. The argument is that all past thinkers were inevitably part of a fast decaying social order and therefore are now suspect because they were trapped in that temporal mode. This argument leads inevitably to relativism, for today's clear-sighted wisdom rapidly becomes yesterday's deception.

There are further reasons for the language of the writers in this volume failing to be admitted to the arena of dialogue. At the heart of the exclusion is the way in which the late twentieth-century dialogue and its terms of reference have been defined in technocratic, utilitarian terms. To a society postulating urgent, and therefore necessarily simple, ends for human action, any activity becomes categorized in one of only two ways: it is either justified by a language of public service or by a language of individual private satisfaction. I believe that Newman and these other writers did not simply choose either of these arguments in the 1930s and 1940s. They were establishing a much more complex and subtle response to the issue of the identity of the university as a place of human activity, with a kind of third force language. The problem is, that it is easy to exclude them from the debate, to shut out of hearing the contribution that they made, because that contribution does not fit the apparently common-sense dichotomy of public and private utility. I am indebted to Geoffrey Price (1985) for a detailed analysis of the distinctions between 'private' and public, corporate solutions.

A technocratic, utilitarian view of society sees a society's institutions serving one end and justifying them on that premise alone. Does an institution support the greater good of the state? If so, a university has to be judged by the same criteria as any other institution in the market for public good. Such measures of value are, again, those of product and performance measured by standards of service to the consumer. A fundamental point is that it is a group external to the university which sets the criteria. We shall find in the chapters that follow that what we might now call 'performance indicators' are proposed by these writers from within the realms of academic life itself. The UK's *White Paper on Higher Education* (DES 1987) is a *locus classicus* of the establishment of such rules and measures, with a rationed, apportioned room for some small extra area of freedom. As Geoffrey Price (1985: 46) states, the culture created can be thus described: 'Order and progress are its mottoes; its role is intended to be benevolent, but its requirements are all-embracing.'

As far as building a philosophy of higher education is concerned, an intriguingly tight situation develops in that culture. Definition and categorization become simplified into stark polar positions. The technocratic society with the moral criteria of the marketplace sets the way in which questions are asked in the debate. So the questions raised are: 'Is the university an agent of the state like other agents?' and 'If it is not, then is it a separate state within a state?' Justification only becomes a problem when the community of shared interest disintegrates and reforms. Similarly, Gellner (1974) argues that discussion of legitimization arises only when law is not shared and understood. You only scramble to get into a boat when you are in the water but not happy to be adrift and unattached. In philosophical terms, the definition has been precluded by the positioning of two possibilities: 'in' (public bodies in the state system) and 'out' (private and outside the state system).

I hope that the chapters which follow will reveal that this simple dichotomy of discussion is a shallow response to human potential. The writers in this volume represent a point of view which is shaded in colour, the universities they propose would be neither of the state nor out of it. Sadly, because they are neither black nor white, they are neglected because they confuse the argument, and therefore they are alleged to be part of a dated past. They are indeed difficult to fit into modern bifocal antagonisms and perplexing in the questions they raise. As I shall try to say later, they in fact propose the questions we have forgotten to ask. One more difficulty for this group of thinkers deserves attention. This attack is from the very shore batteries of philosophy itself.

When a scholar engages in the process of theoretically 'building a university', a great risk is taken, for he or she directly or individually reveals the nature of an ideological base. Show us your ideal university and it will reveal which flag you are hesitating to fly under or even do not know you are waving. Such an attitude leads to a flight from any theory of higher education (see Barnett 1985). Ultimately, this particular line of argument leads to the most destructive erosion of the position of those who attempt to assert anything positive. As Bloom (1987) has so well illustrated, relativism destroys the capacity to hold any personal philosophical positions, other than relativism itself. We shall, however, have to ask genuine questions about relevance as we read each chapter. Where do the writers in this study stand (if they do stand together) and how can they be judged 40 or 50 years on? Has their ideology run dry – is it so thin, over the time past, that their intellectual origins are revealed and found to be appropriate? Are they dated by allegiances that are no longer apposite? Before you tackle each writer individually and make up your own mind, you should be aware that already there are two main antagonistically critical approaches to the twentieth-century writers in this volume, namely the New Right and the neo-Marxist. Both of these, from their very different angles, see these thinkers as inheritors of an alienated ideology. I regret that both schools of thought have not just been armchair theorists reducing schools of thought to intellectual rubble, they have had the effect of closing down discussion by other academics who themselves may be in neither political camp. The rapid popularization of quasi-intellectual movements, both right and left, has helped to confirm in the public eye the categorization that these writers are *passé*. It is perhaps a condemnation of the second half of the century that intellectual fashion, programmed to change, committed to revisionism, should be so triumphant. Let us consider the two wings of criticism as illustrated by two distinguished and widely read writers.

Criticism from the left and right

The Marxist critique of Karl Jaspers and Paul Tillich is one particular window into the house of intellect identified in this study. In *Existentialisme ou Marxisme?*, Lukacs (1961: 109) made one of his most celebrated criticisms of the existentialists: 'L'existentialisme risque de devenir un jour – bien involontairement – l'ideologie de la reaction.'

This charge of reactionary thinking is worth attention, and a few defensive points can be made. I have to concede that the writers we are to consider can hardly withstand the charge of bourgeois origins. Certainly, all write about a special or élite group of the population. It could be held that they write more in terms of an intellectual class than of a social class. Of course, the Marxist riposte might well be that such a surface distinction of intellectual class is only a covering and a transformation of a deeper reality of social class. It is true that all the writers display a bourgeois concentration on occupational status, for what distinguishes them all is the European conception of the learned profession. In the 1930s and 1940s, it is almost taken as an axiom that a major route into the law and medical professions and, to a lesser extent, the clergy, would be through the university system, although a wider definition of the term 'profession', by the embracing of a range of occupations under that title, followed the Second World War. Universities which themselves claim to be the principal centres for professional preparation earn the natural criticism of those who see the professions as the bastions of reaction and privilege. As we shall see, however, each writer's purpose was not to preserve privilege but to enlarge the quality of the contribution of professions to the good society. The traditional professions were to be guardians of liberty who, through their experience as students within the shaping influence of the university, could review and reform civilization.

Although it is possible to quarrel with the soubriquet of 'reactionary', it is even more important to admit that the writers in this volume each represent a form of 'conservatism'. This is a term in fundamental ways different from 'reaction'. They grasped the importance of the continuity of, but not necessarily the immutable nature of, institutions. In some respects, they are exceptional as mid-century thinkers (and certainly some were exceptional as existentialists) in seeking to present a positive philosophy, rather than a social or a political critique of institutions. We have already noted the common criticism of 'inauthentic being' made by their contemporaries, against most public institutions and their representatives. Schools and universities, along with the family and other conservative bodies, were seen by many existentialist writers as well as by Marxists as affected by *mauvais foi*.

In Marxist terms, of course, an even deeper criticism, that of vested interest, is made against the institutions that capitalism created and that, in their turn, sustained capitalism itself. The response to this criticism and the important stand that the writers in this volume took, is that an institution of higher education is the embodiment of civilized forces. The university is cherished, not because of what it was and, in virtually all cases, not because of what it is, but because of what it can be. The view that this old institution, though fatally attracted to control and reaction, is one of society's means of permitting the possibility of social change, never deserted writers represented in this volume. All of them continued to justify their faith in the potential of the traditional institution, despite the saddening experiences of institutional failure in Germany and Spain at the very moment they were writing in the university's defence. This was not reaction, but it is, however, idealism, the idealism that perceived that traditional Western European institutions such as universities have inherent potential for maintaining civilized life. We shall return to that very issue of the value of the institution in the chapters that follow. There is one important fact to be recorded before moving to the opposite pole of political thinking. The left's suspicion of Ortega and Unamuno for what was interpreted as a compromise with Franco's regime explains some of the antagonism to both writers. This slice of history should not concern us. In the event, both thinkers ultimately rejected totalitarianism (for many other reasons than the independence of the university). Recent texts on the politics of Ortega give a more balanced view of these two intellectuals caught in the web of the history of the 1930s (see Dobson 1989; Gray 1989).

Turning to the right-wing critique, we see it very well illustrated by Daniel Bell as the 1960 herald of the emergence of the right in widely read works like *The End of Ideology*. In that work, Bell makes a list of one set of writers of a dying ideology: Ortega, Jaspers, Tillich, Marcel, Lederer and Arendt. Three of them are of course in this volume. In Bell's work, they are at least given credit for influence: 'Marxism apart, it is probably the most influential social theory in the Western World today' (Bell 1960: 21).

Bell refers here to what he calls 'the theory of mass society'. His criticism of these theoreticians is that they oversimplified society and particularly the rich variety of American society. Because they were interested in individual freedom, they paid no regard to the complex public freedoms occurring before their very eyes in a plural society with many forms of social action and many varied social groups. He finds that the ideologies these writers promulgate falsely romanticize organic communities of the past and fail to observe the new growth of communities in modern technological society, and 'no longer serves as a description of modern western society but as an ideology of romantic protest against contemporary life' (Bell 1960: 36).

In addition, Bell loads his critical gun with an even more powerful bullet, namely that the ideologies are sterile in action. Their verve and energy produce no results. They are unable to convert their passion, formerly their undoubted source for action, into a convincing programme for the modern intellectual. For Bell, they fail to excite the new man of the second half of the century because they live in the future. Unlike these thinkers of the past, the modern intellectual belongs to a new consensus on political issues with contemporary goals and satisfactions rather than with far-off ideals for future attainment.

The first thing that strikes the reader, more than 25 years on from the publication of *The End of Ideology*, is how its own ideology is alive and active. It is fascinating to see how the rather vague notions of a practically minded, liberally tolerant, living-for-the-present theory of humanity was transformed step by step into the political action of monetarism and advanced capitalism. The inheritance of this revision of capitalist optimism has been a new dogma: the reduction of state intervention in domestic affairs – yet with a corresponding increase in state intervention in foreign affairs and in some areas of public life, notably in the universities, colleges and schools. In the UK, the ideology of 'pluralism' and freedom of choice has, in the event, led to more legislative intervention and 'steer' to education than at any previous time.

Bell's trenchant criticism of the then dominant perception of 'Mass Man' must, of course, be addressed by anyone reading Ortega y Gasset, Jaspers,

F. R. Leavis and Horkheimer. In my view, a second reading of these writers from the vantage point of the end of the century does not leave one with a sense of a worn-out theme. The features of mass education criticized by Ortega y Gasset, for instance, or regretted by Karl Jaspers or solemnly held up for analysis by F. R. Leavis, are as relevant as they were when first written. It may be true that, when viewed with the brilliant clarity of hindsight, the general social criticism of the writers represented here reads at times as over-simple and even naive. They did not have the advantage of marketing surveys or the anthropological studies of cultures, the intensive 'fieldwork' of the modern social theorist. In many ways, the forecasts of doom that this group of writers predict about the changing aspects of crowded urban life and the disappearing rural scene have been proved wrong in many aspects, but new, complex and deep problems have emerged which they could not have foreseen. In respect of 'plurality' itself, however, there can be no apology made to Bell. This group of writers are, above all, celebrants of the wide variety of human response to learning. All the writers here consider that higher education should be organized to encourage plurality rather than to enforce uniformity. The university is seen as the essential meeting place of differences. Jaspers and Tillich, to name only two, value differences because dialogue takes place across intellectual divides. Newman too rejoices in the variety of all the disciplines in his ideal university.

Insistence on difference and differentiation is of course to fall into Bell's next trap. He alleges that this group of ideologues seeks individual freedom on an aristocratic basis. They are concerned less with general conditions of freedom in society and more with the freedom of the person. The writers here might reply that abstractions such as 'general conditions of freedom' are not things one needs to defend with too much energy, unless in the pursuit of individual freedom there is a consequent inhibition of freedom for another. They would certainly find it puzzling to consider what was so practical about the freedom of a clan or a group in contrast to the individual's freedom within that class or group.

It is in terms of these writers' remoteness from social action that Bell's analysis is, to my mind, most faulty. Every writer we are to consider has taken serious note of the importance of the university, through its participants engaging in social action. Each one, in different ways, endorses that objective. I believe I have illustrated in each case each writer's claims that the university has a vital public role. Although each of their 'mission statements' is based on a view that the ideal university is a powerful influence on public life, the university is not put forward as a crudely operating factor. Indeed, it is at its weakest when it behaves as if it is a pressure group or institutionalized political party. An example of this view is seen in the chapter on Karl Jaspers. He strongly argues that direct engagement with public affairs reduces the university's power to influence society. As they addressed the issue of social action, all of the thinkers in this volume, to varying degrees, considered that the university and its members should be one step removed from political involvement, not in order to absolve themselves from public sins, but to be deeply operating agents of social change and, most valuably, to be channels of social criticism.

It is fascinating that both left and right are similar in criticizing 'the theoreticians' as Bell calls them, from the same two perspectives. These thinkers have been condemned on the one hand because they were judged to be dangerously active, energized by an alleged out-dated or class-based ideology. At the same time, they were judged to be incapacitated from action by virtue of a loss of energy owing to inadequacy of social theory. The two criticisms contradict each other and I hope a reading of these thinkers on the university and its public function will be enough to make a less partisan critic modify his or her judgement on this issue.

Constructing an explanation of the Western European university

Leaving now the two main groups most antagonistic to this group of writers, we must ask if the thinking of these mid-century thinkers will genuinely continue to contribute to the theoretical foundations of the year 2000? My answer is that the thinkers here can justifiably ride the storm of criticism which alleges that their credibility is outworn by time or is damaged by their implicit prejudice. It is possible to evaluate their contribution without the fashionable phobia of 'being dated' and to assert that they continue to make a living contribution to the construction of a philosophy of higher education. The writers must be left to speak for themselves, but before they do so, a number of general points must be made about them.

First, it is vital to interpret the most obvious feature of all seven thinkers: they are Western European thinkers writing about Western European institutions of considerable antiquity. Even Horkheimer, a radical reformist, leading a new institution, is concerned to build that new institution within a well-understood tradition of European academic freedom, with a continuing cultural life distinct from the modern state and with its own grounds of academic justification. The Western European universities have had a unique historical political position. Their peculiarity has been that, at the same time, they have existed within and without the state. In the USA, the history has been very different. Even bearing in mind the land-grant colleges and the state universities, the American experience was, until recently, preponderantly one of private capital and private revenue. In many cases, the image of independence from state or federal funding was jealously preserved, even if, on close examination, it proved to be much more complicated than it appeared to European eyes. So, for instance, the complexities of government research funding, particularly for military purposes, bit hard in that country with its longstanding tradition of academic and local independence. The political history of American higher education was not only markedly different from that of the universities of Western Europe, it has been the one most 'written up' in studies of government and academic freedom. The individuality of the Western European universities and colleges and the significant variations even within one country (particularly in Germany), make generalizations about relationships between academic and government life very difficult. What needs to be said – and the writers here, each by re-telling his own experience, say it – is that the Western European university has been walking a line between a public role and a private independence for a very long time. It was a knife edge particularly sharpened for two of the countries represented in this study, Germany and Spain, when the corporate state bore down upon academic freedom and upon the individual academics who worked within that setting. The academics who were conscious of their broader inheritance of academic freedom were also conscious of their commitment as intellectuals to public life and aware of being in a complex position on a frontier.

It is perhaps this subtle and difficult public position that presents the first building block of a philosophy of higher education as delineated by the thinkers in this volume. Each sees that the university, or in Horkheimer's case, the specialist institution, has held and could continue to hold a critical but constructive role in society. Their understanding of the history of learning in Europe and their consciousness of their inherited academic richness, which was personally and corporately considerable, led them to see the risks of becoming agents of a 'secular' power, but equally stiffened their determination not to build ivory towers. Each chapter shows that social responsibility was always included within their image of the ideal institution of learning.

Two more things need to be said on this particular point. The first is that these writers, although from time to time they may over-claim the value of the university to modern society, are conscious that people outside the university walls do learn, do research, and do attempt to change society and generally to engage successfully in public action. Secondly, they do not claim that the mere presence of an institution, however well organized and however clearly established in its aims and objectives, will of itself hold a mirror up to society. It is the university's influence on the formation of people that effectively acts upon and reflects upon society. Jaspers, for example, is keen to avoid 'character formation' as an objective of the ideal university, but he, like the others, is just as conscious of the shaping force on those who have studied in a civilized institution. These writers take it for granted that the 'humane professions' train their new cadres of recruits through the university system. They are writing at a stage before the debates about how a profession is defined or how a capitalist society sustains and protects its professional classes. Untroubled by such issues, these thinkers martial their arguments, asserting with confidence that one of the university's main functions is to prepare and train new recruits to humane professions by concentrating on their minds and on their humanity rather than on their skills or their technological aptitudes.

The next basis for a philosophy of higher education emerging from the witnesses in this study is the recognition of the university as an institution for the encouragement of diversity. It would be easy to assume from the readings recommended in each chapter that there is a concentration on the notions of unity, wholeness and integration. This emphasis should not blind any reader to the richness of meetings between opposites or to the heady brew of dialectic arising out of the meeting of diverse minds. Even a specialized institution, such as Horkheimer's Frankfurt School, was planned to hold together diverse spheres of study and to cause interaction to take place. In explicit references to what Jaspers called 'boundary situations', we see the potential richness of diversity. Paradoxically, it is because these writers continued to pursue the older philosophical tradition of wholeness and universality that they value distinctiveness and diversity. Even Ortega's doctrine of educational parsimony (Chapter 3), a plea for the concentration of studies, is not a limitation of experience, except in terms of what is humanly graspable. What marks this group as being considerably more than fanciful believers in the romantic pursuit of the universality of knowledge, is their insistence that universities must structure the experience of their students and plan for the meeting of minds. The actual ideal curriculum proposed by most of the writers here may have a quaint and impractical appeal to us now, but the principle behind each was one of a deliberate building of connections rather than of a reliance on good luck and a happy coincidence providing fertile ground for serious study.

We should note that one possible side-effect of reading this material is to feel a boost of spirit, a renewal of a sense of purpose in being engaged in teaching in higher education. To boost a reader's sense of confidence might not seem a very serious objective for a philosopher, but many practising academics would privately agree that thinkers who establish hope require some consideration in the final years of the century. Bear in mind, however, that the hope being considered here is not a false, Utopian variety, for the writers have a conservative stance, and their assurance is not the assurance of dreams or of a therapist's couch. Learning, they would argue, has too often been assumed to be the sponge that takes up the surface energy and excess vigour released in times of affluence or of increased or imposed leisure. In the second half of the century, many arguments for continuing education tend to use the language of gentling the masses. (If 'they' were busy in evening classes, then the under-employed would be more fulfilled and therefore more content.) That is a doctrine of consolatory despair and not a line followed by the seven thinkers here. Take, for example, Unamuno, who most prominently applies a philosophy of last things. He is also the sternest opponent of a doctrine of learning which provides escape from reality. All the thinkers concern themselves with hope and with belief in human potential and the liberating power of learning.

The chapters in this book follow a common pattern. I shall examine a particularly 'key text', where the author considers the nature of higher education, and I shall explain the background for the occasion of the delivery of that text as a speech or written essay. Then I shall try to explain how those specific ideas were supported by or developed in that author's other, usually more well-known, publications. All engage in different ways with very similar enquiries, and therefore each chapter will, to varying degrees according to the individual's chain of logic in setting out his ideas, attempt to cover three persistent themes. The first is the way human learning occurs and, for these writers, the nature of humanity is inevitably linked with it. They all, inevitably, tackle issues about the special duties and particular responsibilities of the intellectual in society, which usually leads to the social role of the university. Some writers emphasize one aspect of learning in higher education rather than another, but there is always an excursion into curricular matters and organizational issues, either explicitly or implicitly, because the ideal university must have content and structure, after all. As they were made painfully aware by personal history, the university may live in the mind but it is trapped in a body of buildings, regulation and structures. Each chapter concludes with a short and highly personal view of what is relevant today from a reading of their work. Finally, there is a chapter setting out the origin of the European debate about higher education and an assessment of the impact of these writers, with a personal note on their significance to at least one participant.

References

Barnett, R. (1985). Higher Education: Legitimisation crisis. *Studies in Higher Education,* **10** (3).

Barzun, J. (1968). *The House of Intellect.* London, Warburg and Secker.

Bell, D. (1960). *The End of Ideology.* New York, Free Press.

Bloom, A. (1987). *The Closing of the American Mind.* New York, Simon and Schuster.

Brubacher, J. S. (1982). *On the Philosophy of Higher Education.* San Francisco, Jossey Bass.

Department of Education and Science (1987). *White Paper on Higher Education.* London, HMSO.

Dobson, A. (1989). *An Introduction to the Politics and Philosophy of José Ortega y Gasset.* Cambridge, Cambridge University Press.

Gellner, E. (1974). *Legitimation of Belief.* Cambridge, Cambridge University Press.

Gray, R. (1989). *The Imperative of Modernity.* Los Angeles, University of California Press.

Kerr, C. (1963). *The Uses of the University.* Cambridge, Mass., Harvard University Press.

Lukacs, G. (1961). *Existentialisme ou Marxisme?* Paris, Nagel.

Price, G. (1985). Universities today: Between the corporate state and the market. *Universities Quarterly,* January, 43–58.

2

J. H. Newman: *The Idea of a University*

Newman's classic text on the idea of the university probably earns more citations in analyses of the modern university than any other work. It is notably an historian's starting block. Other intellectual athletes, planners, politicians and managers of institutions, all refer the reader back to *The Idea of a University*. Occasionally, after a perusal of a range of such works, one has the feeling that the words of Newman can be used to justify most, if not all, positions on higher education. In the one area where there is consensus, there is perhaps the least accuracy. Most writers parade him as the quintessential liberal thinker, whereas 'liberal' was not a word he would have personally espoused, except in the very specific sense of 'liberal educational philosophy'. In his time, liberalism meant liberal theology, the very opposite of Newman's commitment to the authority of the Catholic Church, to which he became a convert in 1845. I have no quarrel, however, with this term in respect of Newman's proposal for a university where academic freedom is unrestrained by external authority and where the subjects (traditionally called the 'liberal arts') flourish alongside science and are distinguished from the 'useful arts'. In these respects, Newman is certainly the touchstone for thinkers in his own time and in our century who foster the idea of a university which has a large generous freedom to develop under its own academic structures and self-imposed constraints. This famous text, the *locus classicus* of ideas of a university, is not only a general model for future thinkers and teachers, it serves us here as a singularly appropriate good example for the key texts of the twentieth-century writers who are reviewed in the following chapters of this volume. There are many similarities between the Victorian theologian's work and the pronouncements of mid-twentieth-century thinking.

The key text: *The Idea of a University*

The Idea of a University began, like most of these key texts, in the form of a public address. John Henry Newman, then a Roman Catholic priest of the Oratory in Birmingham, became Rector of the newly created Catholic University in Dublin in November 1851. The University was newly established by the

Archbishop of Dublin to provide what he and his Church regarded as the only possible alternative to the Anglican Trinity College, where Catholic men could study at a higher level. The first students, 20 in all, arrived in November 1854. By 1858, Newman had resigned from his post, to return to his pastoral duties in Birmingham. Although the Catholic University was still small and ailing financially, the idea that its first Rector generated from the task of establishing that small enterprise, has made it of world importance in the history of institutions. Nine lectures were given, and subsequently published in 1853, in a volume entitled *Discourses on University Education*. Five years later, a second volume was published, with lectures and essays on related subjects, such as 'Christianity and Letters', 'Catholic Literature' and 'Discipline of Mind'. It was 1873 before the edition with the title *The Idea of a University* was published, with the original nine lectures revised and the second part of the volume consisting of revisions of the lectures and essays. The complete text, it has to be said, despite the reverence with which it has been treated since the 1870s, forms two uneven parts. The nine lectures read magnificently and with the impelling movement that had previously made their author a gripping preacher at St Mary's, the University Church at Oxford. The collection in the second half is more dated and uneven in quality and I shall refer only to two essays within it (Newman 1873). Any writer on higher education is in danger of assuming that the readers know as much as they need to about Newman. He is perhaps more often quoted than any other writer on education, but I wonder how many have returned to the text. Those who have will forgive, therefore, the next few paragraphs. I shall summarize the line of argument in the nine discourses and hope that those who know them well will skip them and move on to the key issues which Newman shared with the twentieth-century writers in this volume.

In the first words of the preface to the collection of 1852, Newman sets out his definition of the university simply and clearly. It also defines his use of the word 'idea', that is to say 'an essential end' or object. We shall see in this book, how easy it is to substitute 'ideal' for idea:

> The view taken of a university in these discourses is the following: that it is a place of teaching universal knowledge. This implies that its object is, on the one hand, intellectual, not moral; and on the other, that it is the diffusion and extension of knowledge rather than the advancement. If its object were scientific and philosophical discovery, I do not see why a university should have students; if religious training, I do not see how it can be the seat of literature and science. (Newman 1873: 7.)

In the next chapter, we look at the author who used almost the same title for his text, Karl Jaspers. He too starts with an equally direct statement about the purpose of what really is an 'ideal' university, very different though the situation and the history of the two thinkers had been. Both present themselves to the reader as men with direct opinions based on a life-time of experience of university study, in the mainstream, as it were, of their country's system. In Newman's case, although he may have been addressing a provincial audience, his life-time's almost tangible commitment was to the University of Oxford. In the nine addresses that follow, the experience of that ancient foundation colours all his opinions. The first discourse begins with that experiential insight: that his experience of Oxford was valid for the present task. The first three discourses are in part an argument to justify the application of Protestant experience of universities to the new Catholic university, and so the first discourse ends with Newman's lyrical reminder to his Dublin audience that Irish and English learning had once led the world. A partnership could still be a glowing goal for the future of Catholic learning; there was nothing to fear from Protestant experience. The second discourse remains in the sphere of religious belief. 'Theology as a Branch of Knowledge' is an elaborate and elegant justification for the inclusion of that particular academic discipline in a university's curriculum. We must remember that Newman was writing at a time when in England's new urban centres university colleges were being established, often with a deliberate exclusion of theology. Newman insists in this discourse, and in the third and fourth, that a university must teach 'universal knowledge', and theology is an essential subject in that universality. Partial maps of knowledge are dangerous as well as inadequate. If theology is omitted, another subject will spring into the space it leaves and a biased view of universal truth will result.

The first few discourses are, at one level, practical material designed to reassure a Catholic audience as well as to encourage them and lift their morale. They include, however, nuggets of great value in educational terms, giving insights into Newman's own views of the relationships between subject disciplines, the way in which knowledge is processed by reason in higher education and the value of the university as a comprehensive institution in terms of the spread of human knowledge. It is easy to forget, however, the context in which these opening addresses were written. In fact, Newman is making an impassioned plea for a liberal, generous approach to areas of learning of which the Catholic faithful might have been intensely suspicious.

When we consider discourses V–VII, we enter a more wide-ranging survey of the nature of a university. These are possible to read without the limitations of historical context. Discourse V is perhaps the most often raided for quotations because it is about 'knowledge as its own end'. The important sections on the student experience will be commented upon in later paragraphs. Equally important and equally well known are Newman's distinctions between 'liberal knowledge' and 'useful knowledge'. Newman picks up a point he made in an earlier discourse. Knowledge is called a science or a philosophy when 'it is acted upon, informed, or if I may use a strong figure, impregnated by reason' (Newman 1873: 137). When raised to a higher level by reason, knowledge becomes very powerful and 'has a result beyond itself':

> I know well it may resolve itself into an art, and terminate in a mechanical process, and in tangible fruit; but it also may fall back upon that reason which informs it, and resolve itself into philosophy. In one case it is called useful knowledge, in the other liberal. (Newman 1873: 137)

Discourse VI proceeds to examine further the relation of knowledge to learning and thereby returns to the function and purpose of a university. To

Newman, the chief function is 'intellectual culture'. As with knowledge itself, so with the cultivation of the intellect, useful results may ensure. The educated mind has acquired power and may be of inestimable value to society. How these powers are generated occupies a significant, indeed famous, passage where Newman places trust in the almost mysterious effect of the community of learning. This passage is worth repeating even for the clauses of qualification within it. Even more, it is of historical importance because it has acted as the clarion call for many English institutions, relying as they have on the values of a residential institution:

> I protest to you, Gentlemen, that if I had to choose between a so-called university, which dispensed with residence and tutorial superintendence, and gave its degrees to any persons who passed an examination in a wide range of subjects, and a university which had no professors or examinations at all, but merely brought a number of young men together for three or four years, and then sent them away as the University of Oxford is said to have done some sixty years since, if I were asked which of these two methods was the better discipline of the intellect mind, I do not say which is *morally* the better, for it is plain that compulsory study must be a good and idleness an intolerable mischief – but if I must determine which of the two courses was the more successful in training, moulding, enlarging the mind, which sent out more men the more fitted for their secular duties, which produced better public men, men of the world, men whose names would depend on posterity, I have no hesitation in giving the preference to that university which did nothing over that which exacted of its members an acquaintance with every science under the sun. (Newman 1873: 165)

The theme of usefulness to society continues into Discourse VII. A university education is 'a diffusing good, or as a blessing, or a gift or a power, or a treasure' which the owner possesses but then through him passes to the world at large. I shall return to the theme of the university and its relationship with the wider world in a later paragraph. The last two sections of this discourse, however, should be read by those who like poetic prose and, in particular, by those who can accept a near ecstatic style. It is in these sections that Newman sings the virtues of the gentlemen of intellect, possessing gifts of a rare and elevated character.

Discourses VIII and IX return again to the religious issues. The question of religion and science and their uneasy relationship in a Catholic institution is carefully considered. Strangely enough, these passages are often neglected when Newman's thesis is extolled as a pattern for twentieth-century institutions. Here Newman, the moral teacher, is, at least initially, at his most severe. Science and literature are both 'dangerous' to the Church; science because it ignores 'moral evil', literature because it is wholly concerned with it. Literature must be about the real world and the real world is a place of evil. The answer, however, is not to exclude science and literature, nor to invent a Catholic science and a Catholic literature. That strategy would change their essential nature and create something new and less scholarly. Newman's typically 'liberal' conclusion is clear: the Church's principle is:

> . . . one and the same throughout: not to prohibit truth of any kind, but to see that no doctrines pass under the name of truth but those which claim it rightfully. (Newman 1873: 238)

So the discourses are completed on a high generous note of inclusion, not of exclusion. The Church and its mission, however, remains over and above the noble, yet ultimately inferior world of higher learning.

The final essays, added after the discourse, elaborate further on the issues of Church and science and Church and literature. Three are on science, three on literature. Although they contain great statements of liberal education buried within them, they have rightly not deserved the attention of the original discourses themselves. I commend, however, the lectures on 'Christianity and Scientific Investigation' and 'Discipline of Mind', an address to evening classes. Newman was nothing if not consistent and these essays confirm or elaborate the views of the discourses. I shall refer to them in the paragraphs that follow, which examine three perennial themes also found in the thinkers of the twentieth century who directly or indirectly owed much to Newman's original text.

Knowledge and learning: The human process

It will be a consistent theme of this book that writers who think about higher education base their assumptions of how people learn on a theory of knowledge, which in its turn is part and parcel of their theory of human nature. Some writers demonstrate a clear, logical ladder of abstraction from a practical proposal of an ideal curriculum up through the organization of knowledge, on to their definition of what is entailed by being human. Others are more mysterious about this chain of thought and it has to be teased out from a range of their written works. In the case of Newman, the evidence is there before us from the first moment. His starting point is, naturally, a religious one. Humanity is part of the created universe. Jesus Christ gives us the perfect example of Man, and the relationship between human beings and God is the only feature of life that ultimately counts. Newman's theology, despite his insistence on the importance of reason in relation to knowledge, is a long way beyond eighteenth-century deism. He is a descendant of the Romantic Revolution, but also and more significantly someone who has been a pilgrim back beyond the Middle Ages to the Early Fathers and the Church of the Acts of the Apostles. This complex inheritance, through theology, does not, however, exclude him from the mainstream of nineteenth-century thought on the nature of knowledge. The consonance of his writing on the nature of understanding and of faith with the thinking of Coleridge has been observed by many, although Basil Willey (1964) is correct to remind us that Newman did not read Coleridge until 1838. What identified Newman as a man of his own time, along with Coleridge and Matthew Arnold, is the emphasis upon the wholeness of the human being. They saw a complex of the intellectual, moral and aesthetic senses as well as the traditional physical senses, and, in Newman's case, with a religious presence. The simple division of subject and object, receiver and sensation, is no longer adequate. The internal ordering of experience is the pre-eminent feature in the human psychology of this generation, and from this standpoint they say much, not only about the obvious nature of sensory knowledge, but also about how we encounter other kinds of knowledge and what we do with it in the processes of learning.

It should also be recorded that Newman is profoundly faithful to the idea of reason, believing that it is a gift, a kind of grace which enables knowledge to be used to effect. In Discourse IV, there is an explanation, not untypical of much earlier writers of the end of the eighteenth century, on the mental processing of sense experiences. Like Coleridge, Wordsworth, Joseph Priestley and Humphry Davy (to cover the spectrum of literature and sciences), Newman talks in terms of an active universe. Unlike the beasts, Newman says, the intellect of Man does not merely receive sights and sounds. To use his own terminology, he 'energizes', 'seizes and unites' and 'sees in sights and sounds something beyond them'. More significantly even, human beings perceive beauty 'and what is not' and give sensations 'a meaning and invests them with an idea' (Newman 1873: 107). This particular disquisition then leads into an analysis of the errors that follow the almost automatic human urge to create form out of sense impressions. Error in particular arises out of partial experience or out of the narrow specialization of one subject of study, such as one of the sciences. Again, wholeness is all. As Newman wrote in the third discourse:

> . . . I lay it down that all knowledge forms one whole because its subject matter is one; for the university in its length and breadth is intimately knit together that we cannot separate off portion from portion and operation from operation, except by mutual abstraction. (Newman 1873: 87)

The Creator, of course, is the force of unity in all aspects of his creation. As Newman says in the fifth discourse on 'knowledge its own end':

> I have said all branches of knowledge are connected together because the subject matter of knowledge is intimately united in itself, as being the acts and the work of the Creator. (Newman 1873: 127)

So far, we have assumed that there are two simple components – activated experience reassured by reason – in Newman's epistemelogical armoury. If that were the case, then we are remarkably close to a mechanical explanation of the processes of learning. Such a logical chain of operation of the human mind in action would not have been too foreign to the eighteenth-century mind. A more detailed explanation of the processes that, through the action of reason in knowledge, lead to truly liberal learning occurs in Discourse V. Knowledge is acted upon, 'informed' and 'impregnated' by reason. This action is an unmasking or an illuminating process. In the second section of *The Idea of a University*, entitled 'Discipline of Mind', Newman writes of that impact as being:

analogous to that of a blind man towards the objects of vision, at the moment when eyes are for the first time given to him by the skill of the operator. (Newman 1873: 445)

This is no mere addition of one ingredient to another, it is an 'exaltation' of knowledge. The terms, now so familiar in education – 'culture of the mind' and 'cultivate the intellect' – enter the discourses frequently from this point, giving an explanation beyond the mechanical ones of sense perception and mental ordering of received objects. Although, he continues in the fifth discourse, a person may make use of this higher type of knowledge, he or she may equally well not do so, in which case it becomes truly liberal or 'philosophical knowledge'. The attention of the argument then turns away from knowledge in itself to the possessor and what happens to him or to her. Philosophical knowledge is 'a habit, a personal possession, and an inward endowment'. Here, and in the essay *Discipline of Mind*, the term 'formation of the mind' summarizes the inner changes that occur in a maturing person. Perhaps nothing can give the flavour of a piece of Newman's argument than a longer quotation:

But education is a higher word; it implies an action upon our mental nature, and the formation of a character; it is something individual and permanent, and is commonly spoken of in connection with religions and virtue. When, then, we speak of the communication of knowledge as being education, we thereby really imply that knowledge is a state or condition of mind, and since cultivation of mind is surely worth seeking for its own sake, we are thus brought once more to the conclusion, which the word 'liberal' and the word 'philosophy' have already suggested, that there is a knowledge which is desirable, though nothing come of it, as being of itself a treasure, and a sufficient remuneration of years of labour. (Newman 1873: 139)

Newman tries hard to impress upon his reader at this point that liberal knowledge does not make men better or more religious. Philosophy, he adds a little later in a typically striking section, has no command over the human passions:

Quarry the granite rock with razors, or moor the vessel with a thread of silk; then may you hope with such keen and delicate instruments as human knowledge and human reason to contend against those giants, the passion and the pride of man. (Newman 1873: 145).

Despite these disclaimers, the reader has to observe that in the same discourse, 'liberal education makes not the Christian, not the Catholic, but the gentleman' (Newman 1873: 144). Undoubtedly, the 'gentleman' academic has undergone a vital change of character in the process of learning. The clue to the nature of the process is in the words 'culture' or 'civilization' of the intellect. The process is one like that of the wise agriculturalist, with slow processes of nurture and husbandry, and tended growth in a context of care and watchfulness which takes time and concentration. Its aim may be excellence of the intellect (and not moral virtue at an excelling level), but the process is not so single and unified as it might appear at first reading. Newman is at pains to distinguish religious salvation from the peak of academic effort. As Owen Chadwick (1983: 56) comments: 'Noone ever sang a lovelier song in praise of education for its own sake. And in the same moment noone ever denied so elegantly its natural crown.'

Illuminative reason

It is at this problem-filled juncture that Newman takes up a new discourse, the sixth, and presses on with his argument about learning. Having established that the 'cultivation of the intellect' is sufficient unto itself, Newman continues to examine what happens during that process of cultivation. The two significant words are in the clause 'it is an enlargement or illumination'. The process is an imaginative one shedding light and changing the events on which light is shed, not a mechanical switch revealing what is already waiting to be unfolded. The common view is that learning is an accumulation of knowledge, for we see this process at work in the education of the child. The university, however, operates in a different manner. Although it is a common sense to base all learning experience on an increase of knowledge, philosophy goes beyond the mere acquisition of facts. The process is, again, one of energy and of action. The figures of speech in this discourse are about an active process. Words like 'locomotion', 'movement onwards' and 'culture of the mind' are used to lead to the point where Newman can define the special nature of reason in this sphere of learning. This he calls 'illuminative reason':

> To have even a portion of this illuminative reason and true philosophy is the highest state to which nature can aspire in the way of intellect. (Newman 1873: 159)

The same high-toned note is struck in the lecture, *Discipline of Mind*. Something more is required than acquisition of facts; the process is dynamic:

> Something more than merely admitting it [knowledge] in a negative way into the mind is necessary if it is to remain there. It must not be passively received, but actually and actively entered into, embraced, mastered. The mind must go halfway to meet what comes to it from without: . . . You have come to make what you hear your own by putting out your hand, as it were, to grasp it and appropriate it. You do not come merely to hear a lecture or to read a book, but you come for that catechetical instruction, which consists in a sort of conversation between your lecturer and you. He tells you a thing, and he asks you to repeat it after him. He questions you, he examines you, he will not let you go till he has proof, not only that you have heard, but that you know. (Newman 1873: 440)

This quotation contains two elements which we shall find in other writers in this volume: a predisposition of a committed mind creating a higher form of reasoning necessary for the full process of learning in higher education, and a teaching relationship of dialogue and questioning. This second feature in Newman's case I shall pursue later in the chapter, but, before doing so, I must complete the picture of this higher form of reasoning with commitment. I shall do this by reference to later works by Newman and I shall attempt to fill out what is half-revealed in the sixth discourse and elsewhere in *The Idea of a University* about the nature of this active engagement of the ideal learner.

The word that became more and more significant for Newman in his lectures and writing after his conversion to Rome in 1845 was 'assent'. It was more than a word, he had to live with its full meaning and with the challenges of others who attacked his actions, his arguments for his conversion and even his motives. Although what he came to call 'the grammar of assent' (using 'grammar' in the sense of the underlying forms or structures of belief, just as there are forms and structures underlying a language) was applied not to higher learning but to the act of belief in Church and God, it is possible to identify clear indications of the same subtle process in *The Idea of a University*. We have already seen the components of the qualified, developed form of reason that should apply in a liberal education. The process is 'illuminating'. It progresses in the way that 'cultivation' implies; it is not single-minded, except in determination, but draws on a wide range of studies and, above all, it encourages characteristic qualities of mind. One feature which was implicit in *The Idea of a University* is that of commitment. The student must give all his powers to the process of learning. One part of him (say the intellect) will not suffice. Learning demands the full range of human sensibility. It is this issue of full commitment of the whole person which is developed in later works such as *An Essay in Aid of a Grammar of Assent* (Newman 1870).

As Owen Chadwick (1983: 5) has commented, Newman is, above all, a consistent thinker, although his ideas were elaborated from publication to publication. Chadwick also provides a valuable guide to the connection between the questioning work of reason and the assertive action of faith. Science and history provide argument and questioning to which Catholics must attend with all their rational powers. However, faith cannot be overturned by rational arguments, for they are partial, whereas faith has a vision by 'assent' of the whole scheme of things. Newman uses the term the 'illative sense' for

> the act of assent in the mind based upon a body of grounds in their totality, even though the mind is not aware of all the grounds treated as separate arguments, and may be resting on half-inarticulate experience as well as argument. (Chadwick 1983: 36).

It is 'assent' which converts an 'accumulation of probabilities into certitude'. Readers of the previous paragraphs will also identify a close connection between 'illuminative reason' and the illative sense.

If it is possible to simplify and thence misinterpret Newman's theory of assent, it is not a *Kierkegaardian* 'leap of faith', ignoring rationally acquired truths. As Coulson (1981) explains with great insight. Newman at times appears to require a combination of both types of truth. The 'grammar' of assent is not a 'leap of faith', but a process varying with the person, reaching an ultimate personal climax of assent. Like Coleridge, Newman asks his readers to abandon reductionism. Philosophical systems which make life simple or un-puzzling are dangerous. The Catholic intellectual has to live with uncertainties. The 'faculty' (if it is a faculty) that must be satisfied is not reason, although reason is required to be an active partner, but imagination. Imagination is an intensive, unifying power which makes us give whole-hearted 'energetic' and real assent, 'as if we saw'.

This excursion into what was to Newman primarily, but not exclusively, the domain of religious belief, is important in the understanding of the process of learning which the ideal student should undertake. Are there clues in the *Idea of a University* leading to this broader sense of verification of experience or is *The Idea* built on the assumption that learning in a university (or indeed in any human institution) goes on at a lower level of activity?

I believe that, explicit in Newman's distinction in Discourse VII between a liberal and a useful education, there is a clear indication of the process involving the full commitment of human resources. In a university, Newman argues, the specialist lawyer, medical man, geologist or economist will come to his special area of knowledge, 'as it were, from a height, he has taken a survey of all knowledge, . . . he has gained from than a special illumination and largeness of mind and freedom and self-possession' (Newman 1873: 182). Again, he uses the term 'culture of the intellect'. We shall find in the twentieth-century writers in the following chapters two similar basic beliefs about the education of a complex mind by the processes of higher education. As with Newman, there is actual concentration on 'wholeness' and, secondly, on what is contained in the phrase 'culture of the intellect' – the university is a nurturing institution. As Newman so famously put it, a university is not a foundry, or a mint or a treadmill. We shall next pass on to discern how Newman, in *The Idea of a University*, saw the maternal university actually operating to provide the habitat for the culture of the mind.

The idea of the academic community: The form of the university

The above sketch of Newman's view of knowledge leads us, as it led him, to commend an organization that would encourage wholeness and the avoidance of specialization or of partial, distorted views of the created universe. There are practical difficulties in gaining an all-round perspective. How can students study every abstraction and every science? In the fifth discourse, Newman makes an interesting, indeed ingenious, defence at one and the same time, of breadth and depth of study. Undue prominence to any one science, for instance, will work against the unity of the sciences, which are so interdependent on one another. Again, individual subject disciplines can lead different people to different conclusions. Newman instances the study of the classics in England which have refined taste, but, in France, they have encouraged deistical and revolutionary movements. One area of study needs 'the safeguard', as I may call it of others. However, practical issues arise. Although the range of studies should be extensive in the university, the students 'cannot pursue every subject which is open to them'. The answer is that they must live 'among those and under those who represent the whole circle. This I conceive to be the advantage of a seat of universal learning, considered as a place of education' (Newman 1873: 128). The process is one of respecting, consulting and aiding – in short an ideal community of scholars. The language Newman uses is indicative of his view of the extra-rational means of learning in such a community:

> Thus is created a pure and clear atmosphere of thought, which the student also breathes, though in his own case he only pursues a few sciences out of the multitude. (Newman 1873: 129)

The result is the production of the philosophical habit of mind which is the 'special fruit' of the education furnished at a university. The 'hidden curriculum', as it became known 100 years or more afterwards, is therefore as essential a feature of the idea of Newman's university as the explicit curriculum.

The underlying model is, inevitably, the Oxford college. The Oxford of 1850 was what we would now call a small university, including small residential communities. Its two principal features were the systems of tutorial teaching within a required period of residence. It is not true that there was any unanimity within the University about the value of this system. As earlier comments have indicated, both Oxford and Cambridge were riven by debates about the comparative values of the university and collegiate systems of learning, with the apparently successful examples of German universities hovering over the two ancient English institutions. Contention apart, Newman knew what he had experienced and, furthermore, he had experienced it for a long time and in the depth of his being. Owen Chadwick suggests that Newman's education and his career in Anglicanism and Catholicism always took place in some kind of monastic institution. At school in Ealing, later as a student at Trinity College, Oxford, as a don at Oriel, then into the priests' houses and the Oratory, he was always at home in the small community of common purpose. Such a community was, of course, much more than a domestic arrangement. Its daily rhythms and rituals occupied the whole being of the participants. It is this committed belongingness that pervades Newman's views of the ideal educational context. This is why he could use the figure of speech of 'breathing in' the educational atmosphere in the quotation above. Similarly, it is a mysterious environment which will bring into life other powers which otherwise would not awaken to aid and assist the power of teaching:

> It will give birth to a living teaching, which in course of time will take the shape of a self-perpetuating tradition, or a *genuis loci*, as it is sometimes called, which haunts the home where it has been born, and which imbues and forms, more or less, and one by one, every individual who is successively brought under its shadow. Thus it is that, independent of direct instruction on the part of superiors, there is a sort of self-education in the

academic institutions of Protestant England; a characteristic tone of thought, a recognised standard of judgement is found in them, which, as developed in the individual who is submitted to it, becomes a source of strength to him, both from the distinct stamp it impresses on his mind, and from the bond of union which it creates between him and others – effects which are shared by the authorities of the place, for they themselves have been educated in it, and at all times are exposed to the influence of its ethical atmosphere. (Newman 1873: 167)

This, one of the less familiar passages on the collegiate system, could not be bettered for a description of the conservative, self-directing institution. Its power and influence were felt beyond the mind into the heart. Newman was to write in 1864 in his *Apologia pro Vita Sua* not merely of the knowledge taught by the eminent scholars in his Oxford college but of its emotional meaning. The *Apologia*, written to defend his personal reputation against the attack of Charles Kingsley, reveals consistently how important in the development of Newman's mind were the day-by-day contacts provided by the courts and gardens, by the ordinary human traffic of the university. The Reverend William James taught him the doctrine of the Apostolic Succession 'in the course of a walk, I think round Christ Church meadow'. Dr Whateley, head of Oriel College, 'in the course of a walk' talked with him about a crucial work, *Letters on the Church by an Episcopalian*. He remembered the impact of first seeing Keble 'Walking in the High with a friend'. Indeed, it is the emotional recollection of regularity in the life of the university and the college that produces the insights into learning years later. Writing of his early days as a young don, first beginning to preach and to teach at Oriel College he says, 'It was to me like the feeling of spring weather after winter, and, if I may so speak, I came out of my shell' (Newman 1912: 40).

One final, much more down-to-earth point about the form of the university: Newman envisaged a generous range of subject disciplines. Indeed, the heart of his definition of the constitution of a university as an organization was the word 'universal'. Strangely enough, in Chapter 8 we shall see Unamuno playing with the words 'university' and 'universe'. Newman's argument for the admission of theology into the curriculum was also an argument for all sciences. We now realize that he had no concept of the growth and proliferation of subject divisions or the inclusion of subjects (such as English literature; never mind accountancy or forestry) into the university's portfolio. Nevertheless, we must give him full benefit of his own argument. Newman's university was a generous one. It is sometimes misread as 'the liberal university', in the sense of the American 'liberal arts college', but this was not in Newman's mind. For example, a considerable proportion of the third discourse, 'Bearing of Theology on other Branches of Knowledge', is concerned with the nature of 'material sciences'. The seventh address attached to the original lectures is concerned with 'Christianity and Physical Science', and it took place in the new university's school of medicine. What he wished to establish was that the two spheres of thought, natural and supernatural knowledge, were compatible and capable, nay essential, in being included within the structures of the university. A university which was partial might as well be a specialist institution devoted to a material end, but it could never be Newman's university.

The university and the world

In reading *The Idea of a University*, it is easy to be carried forward by the wonderful rhetoric of the famous fifth discourse and assume that since 'Knowledge Its own End' is the axiom, then the university exists for its own end. It is also easy to assume that the Oxford of the mid-nineteenth century was untroubled by political issues which have haunted our own times. Although there is an element of truth in both assumptions, they do not tell the whole story. Newman had a view about the external purpose of studies in the university. Furthermore, he lived at a time when there was a public debate about higher education. We shall explore this context in the concluding chapter of this book. For the moment, let us concentrate on Newman's own stand on a threatening situation.

In the first place, the Oxford of Newman's time had 'enjoyed' a fair share of external 'interference', although we might think that such pleasures are restricted to our own times. He himself was vigorously involved with the issues of the admission of dissenters into Oxford and Cambridge in the 1830s. Speaking, then, from an Anglican pulpit, he joined those who spoke passionately against a change, or, as his party saw it, a betrayal of the traditional alignment of Church of England and ancient university. Furthermore, he and many others objected to the role Parliament took in the affairs of the university. By mid-century, further battles were to be fought, although Newman himself had left the field for others to defend the universities against Royal Commissions. As the preparatory remarks to this volume indicate, the nineteenth-century institutions were forced into arguments of public justification and into defending their academic independence, not as much perhaps as in our own times, but with the familiar lines being drawn up and the now well-worn arguments then freshly deployed. In all these arguments it is clear where Newman stands. As he said in the first discourse, he had lived in a period when 'an independent body of men setting about a work of self-reformation' (Newman 1873: 47) had succeeded in accomplishing reform. There is no evidence to suggest that Newman thought that they needed any extra help from the state in their task.

If the university has to keep the state at arms' length, what must be its attitude to the Church? This is a particularly thorny problem, so it is not surprising that *The Idea of a University* is occupied (and the word is valid in respect of the amount of time he has to take up with the issue) with the relationship between the Roman Catholic Church and the independence of the university. In this respect, Newman has much to say on 'external relations'. The burden of his argument, about the nature of theology, its relationship with the other subjects in the curriculum and the processes of learning, leads to his conclusion that the Church has no need to fear learning. Much of the book is taken up with arguments of reassurance. There is, however, more to the relationship than independence. In the preface of 1852, for instance, he spells out the political position of both parties:

> Such is a university *in essence*, and independently of its relation to the Church. But, practically speaking, it cannot fulfill its object duly, such as I have described it, without the Church's assistance: or, to use the theological terms, the Church is necessary for its *integrity*. Not that its main characters are changed by this incorporation: it still has the office of intellectual education; but the Church steadies it in the performance of that office. (Newman 1873: 7)

This is the political counterpart of the doctrine of learning which we considered above. As 'assent' is required to reach certitude, but reason is left free to test the stages of intellectual development; therefore, in institutional terms, the Church 'steadies' the university but leaves it free to fulfil its distinct purposes.

Newman has no doubt that the Church will benefit from this arrangement based on freedom and trust. Indeed, in his view, society as a whole will enjoy the fruits of the university. The result of the learning process is not the production of specialized professionals for society's needs, but something much more valuable. The answer here is the word a 'gentleman'. This is such a difficult concept for the world of 1990 to accept that we have to step back to Newman's elaboration of the qualities of a gentleman to grasp what society can receive from this person. We have to put aside very consciously the experience, the criticisms and, yes, the prejudices about social class after years of social change in order to accept the term in a discussion. This is, however, what he believes will emerge:

> 'Good' indeed means one thing, and 'useful' means another, but I lay it down as a principle, which will save us a great deal of anxiety, that, though the useful is not always good, the good is always useful. Good is not only good, but reproductive of good; this is one of its attributes; nothing is excellent, beautiful, perfect, desirable for its own sake, but it overflows, and spreads the likeness of itself all around it. (Newman 1873: 180)

Therefore, the qualities that produce what Newman calls 'health' in the culture of the mind (thinking, reasoning, comparing, discriminating, analysing, and so on) are useful for society. He is confident that a man of intellect can take up any science or profession for which he has a 'taste or special talent with an ease, a grace, a versatility, and a success to which another is a stranger' (Newman 1873: 182). The role of the intellect as a high calling is never better or so simply expressed than in the following passage from the seventh discourse:

> There is a duty we owe to human society as such, to the state to which we belong, to the sphere in which we move, to the individuals to whom we are variously related, and whom we successively encounter in life; and that philosophical or liberal education, as I have called it, which is the proper

function of the university, if it refuses the foremost place to professional interests, does but postpone them to the formation of a citizen, and, while it observes the larger interests of philanthropy, prepares also for the successful prosecution of those merely personal objects, which at first sight it seems to disparage. (Newman 1873: 183)

The inheritance

What can we retain of Newman's clear and, at times, staggeringly confident vision? I have commented elsewhere on the remarkable continuation of his influence into the late twentieth century. It is remarkable in one sense, but in another it is explicable by the fact that his ideas have, for many, consonance with their own reality. What Newman says is what we want to hear about higher education at best. I count myself as one of his most ardent listeners, as perhaps I have implied in earlier paragraphs; nevertheless, there have to be critical comments made about the idea of a university in his terms.

In the first place, there is a considerable difficulty for many academics, and above all for those outside higher education, in accepting Newman's notion of assent in learning. Sadly, for many students and tutors alike, the model for a psychology of learning is closer to the machine than to the complex soul. There is a different, and to me a lower, sense of commitment in some modern solutions to the challenge of growth and increased access. The idea, for instance, of a degree course by credit transfer from a number of institutions is the opposite of Newman's ideal. The accumulation of credits from a variety of subject disciplines may, and indeed does, have much to commend it on grounds of 'utility', to keep to Newman's language. It seems a world apart from Newman's idea of a continuous growing commitment within one place and one sustained period of commitment. It may be that Newman himself set aside the knowledge he undoubtedly possessed of the medieval scholar who visited a variety of Western European institutions. If he did, it was in favour of rootedness and rootedness may be so unacceptable to the new European that his model of learning is out of tune with our times. Newman's doctrine of how we learn, like that of some other authors in this volume, is a complex theory of learning which does not accord with the behaviourist principles of learning (e.g. underlying computer-based learning). So much of modern self-instructional learning is commended on the grounds of economy or of efficient learning psychology. Newman's learning theory depends on dialogue and place, on the scholar who responds not to himself or to herself (or to what has been planned remotely and displayed on a visual display screen) but to others who share the commitment. In brief, Newman's 'fault' for our times is not merely his language with its high tone and noble ambition for the human mind. The language he uses indicates the message which, at heart, is based on a different concept of how people learn as well as what they learn.

A second difficulty must also lie in the changed and diverse nature of modern institutions of higher education. The Oxford college is notably no longer the norm. It is not even continuing in Oxford, despite a remarkable persistency, in a form that Newman would have recognized. The university has grown into a very large institution, by British standards. The departmental structure and the development of scientific and research institutions has changed out of recognition and research has become much more significant than in 1840. Even more, collegiate life has changed. Perhaps it is more accurate to say that what has changed is how collegiate life is viewed by its participants. After years of sociological and anthropological study, particularly but not exclusively in the USA, it is difficult to accept that the student experience of higher education in a collegiate atmosphere is as beneficial to higher learning as Newman said it was (see, for instance, the summary of cultural studies in Becher 1984; Stone 1983: 27). Here there is a clash of a cultural, anthropological view of higher education and, in Newman's case, an ideal view of what he knew to be the case 'at best'. It is not for us to cast doubt from our position of lofty modernity on the validity of Newman's own student experience. What is difficult, however, is to apply the essential thesis of his work, the aim of a community of learning, to the dispersed, varied social institutions of a modern technological society and to say, 'that is what actually happens in our time'. I hope to return to this point in the conclusion of this book.

Finally, the political setting of Newman's university has to be interpreted and measured against the structures of our own times. Newman was obviously writing of an institution, despite the qualifications made in a previous paragraph, at arms' length from central government. He cannot give us direct theoretical guidance on the complex relationship of the government and university of today. The other writers in this book are closer to the grim realities of that relationship. What is worth observing, however, is that he can remind us of who 'owns' higher education. In his language, it is without doubt the men who keep the torch of learning alight. He was able to speak confidently of the value of a liberal education because there was a consensus between the university and the state on the qualities of leadership required in government and the professions. Newman's own term, 'gentlemen', tells it all. Obviously, no such simple accord exists now. Nevertheless, there are phrases and whole paragraphs about the training of character that create echoes with statements made by modern management 'experts' about the desirable personality types for tomorrow's leaders. They have a utilitarian view of such characteristics. For example, they look for the creation of openness to further training and the ability to adapt to change. Their objective is the 'creative thinker'. Newman, however, was operating in a different framework, a moral realm. The successful student was a 'good' man, who benefited a society which shared with him good intentions. Newman assumed the continuity of 'the good' between governed and government of which this century is more sceptical.

Two features are, however, well worth retaining during the subsequent discussion. One is the phrase he uses about the Catholic Church, which aims 'to steady' the university in its performance. I believe that this is a good definition for any Secretary of State for Education to ponder. Secondly, Newman establishes for future discussion, a weighty and vital principle, namely that the university is worthy of most serious consideration because it is an institution inextricably related to time. It is an ancient institution like the Catholic Church and, in Newman's sense of values, that distinction is crucial. Continuity is fundamental. The university is not a machine that can be reassembled elsewhere. The *genuis loci* will disappear in such a pragmatic, crude conceptualization of higher learning. The place itself matters. Newman's own personal continuity was deeply affected by his own conversion. Leaving the Church of England was only one aspect of a tearing up of his own history in 1845. He had assumed that Oxford would be a life-time's commitment. Writing in *The Apologia* about his own undergraduate college as he prepared to leave Oxford for Rome, he composed a poignant 'envoi'. It says more than he knew, not only about his loss, but also about the way that universities and colleges take on a larger and longer life for their alumni than the short period of residence of student days:

> There used to be much snapdragon growing on the walls opposite my freshman's rooms there, and I had for years taken it as the emblem of my own perpetual residence even unto death in my own University. (Newman 1912: 214)

References

Becher, A. (1984). The disciplinary shaping of the profession. In Clark B. R. (ed.) ·*Perspectives on Higher Education*, Berkeley, University of California Press.

Chadwick, O. (1983). *Newman*. Oxford, Oxford University Press.

Clark, B. R. (Ed.) (1987). *The Academic Profession: National, Disciplinary and Institutional Settings*, pp. 271–303. Berkeley, University of California Press.

Coulson, J. (1981). *Religion and the Imagination: In aid of a 'Grammar of Assent'*. Oxford, Clarendon Press.

Newman, J. H. (1870). *An Essay in Aid of a Grammar of Assent* (edited by I. Ker). Oxford, Oxford University Press (reprinted 1985).

Newman, J. H. (1873). *The Idea of a University*. New York, Doubleday (reprinted 1959).

Newman, J. H. (1912). *Apologia pro Vita Sua*. London, J. M. Dent.

Stone, L. (1983). Social control and intellectual excellence. In *Universities, Society and the Future*. Edinburgh, Edinburgh University Press.

Willey, B. (1964). *Nineteenth Century Studies*. Harmondsworth, Penguin.

3

José Ortega y Gasset: *Mission of the University* – 'An Uplifting Principle in the History of the Western World'

The civil-war agony of modern Spain was well and truly in preparation by 1930. At the start of the decade, there was a virtual dictatorship which was beginning to fail, a wobbling monarchy and increasingly ominous civil divisions. The University of Madrid was not exempt from excitement and fear. In that time of crisis, the Spanish Students' Union Federation invited the Professor of Metaphysics of the university to address them in an atmosphere which must have been highly volatile. José Ortega y Gasset had studied in Germany but returned to academic life in what he and many others recognized as a moribund university system out of touch with European academic developments and increasingly dominated by authoritarian government or, almost worse, by the fear of it. Ortega was, however, respected as an exceptional teacher and he had a popular following as a professor. The speech he gave to the assembled students confirmed his reputation with them. It was immediately published in a sequence of newspaper articles, thus widening the circulation of ideas, and finally emerged in book form. The public attention it received was, for many years, largely confined to Spain itself, and was soon to be swallowed up in the larger crisis that was to drown Spain in the long, costly civil war, in which one of the earliest casualties was the freedom of the university system. One of the later authors in this volume, Miguel de Unamuno, was to end his days in virtual house arrest after an outspoken defence of freedom in Spain after the outbreak of civil war. Ortega was fortunate to escape from Spain to work in the USA.

Mission of the University was to be reborn as a text with some influence in Anglo-American thinking immediately after the Second World War. A translation by H. L. Nostrand was published in 1946 (Ortega y Gasset 1946), and it was widely referred to in the post-war debate about the expansion of higher education both in the UK and in the USA. In the UK, it had a ready appeal to an influential section of university opinion which was attempting to retain values in the rapidly growing and changing university system. The seminal work by Walter Moberly (1949), *The Crisis in the University*, contains approvingly a number of quotations from Ortega and from *Mission of the University* in particular. Undoubtedly, this work influenced some of the groups who gave evidence to the Robbins Committee which, in greater or lesser degree, influenced higher education in the UK for the next 35 years. The indirect, but traceable, influence of Ortega on certain areas of study in English colleges and universities has not yet been mapped, but it is visible even in a cursory glance at the index of many influential works on higher education in the 1950s and 1960s. That increasingly tenuous thread apart, *Mission of the University* fell into forgetfulness and, as the years pass, has moved further and further back on the shelves of libraries.

Part of the blame for the decline of public interest in Ortega's ideas must inevitably lie at his own door. He is an inspirational writer, much given to metaphor and flashes of vision. Perhaps his style has been too florid for anxious Northern thinkers. As his close friend and student J. Marias says: 'Metaphors accompany Ortega's prose from the very first page.' And in a striking phrase from Ortega himself, comparing his language with objective language, the author's is like 'The sun throwing off immovable reflections from life's materials arranged in a certain way' (Marias 1970: 264 and 265). He is not easily classifiable politically as left or right, being therefore easily criticized by both extremities. His 'successful' works, *The Revolt of the Masses* and *The Dehumanization of Art*, have shone so brightly that his other writings, including judgements on educational matters, have been put into the shadows. Eventually, his reputation for modern studies of the Press and of aesthetics waned somewhat as the more sophisticated sub-profession of 'media studies' emerged as a fully fledged university and college course. Despite all this weight of neglect, the lapse of time and the inevitable dating from which his writing suffers, he does present a challenge to thinkers about the nature of the university and its function. The valuable source of energy for the continuing attraction of Ortega has been the presence of a 'pressure group' of his former pupils in the USA (see, for instance, the work of Mora 1956, Marias 1970, and a major critical work of the 1970s by McClintock 1971).

The key text: *Mission of the University*

The key text, *Mission of the University*, presents all the themes we shall need to bring out into the fresh air again in considering his contribution to the discussion on higher education, but, in my analysis, I shall aim to relate the principal ideas to other more available writings by Ortega.

The first chapter of *Mission of the University* has a typically conservative title, 'A tempered spirit of reform'. Any reader would be struck immediately, however, by the contrast between that title and the tone of the text that follows the argument, for it is radical and distinctly non-reactionary in its view of human potential in the ideal university. The existing university system of Spain is condemned. It is marred by 'slovenliness', and crucially for what I take to be the central value of Ortega's work for us today, he castigates the state for treating a delicate being with clumsy lack of care: 'the lack of all decorum, of all self-respect, of all decency in the state's manner of performing its peculiarly delicate function' (Ortega y Gasset 1946: 32). Ortega is not pessimistic because he does not believe that institutions and governments necessarily condition men. If they wish to do so, men can change socially, but to be effective they must be 'in form'. A social group can be 'in form' as much as an individual can be fit. 'History proceeds very often by jumps', but groups and individuals, properly educated, can make history jump the right way.

Ortega urged his students to reform the Spanish universities on individual lines, not by copying English or German models. He proposed that reform should not begin with university management structures but with the curriculum itself and, most important for our quest of the individuality of his argument, should be steered by a doctrine of pedagogy. The traditional functions of the Spanish universities, which had been the training of the learned professions and scientific research and investigations, would not be abandoned but would follow rather than lead. To accomplish reform, Ortega would create a new central core of the curriculum. The traditional functions would be limited by what could be well taught and by what could be well learned.

The central core of the new university curriculum would be 'culture'. This, says Ortega, is not the 'residue' of general culture, which apparently persisted in the University of Madrid's contemporary courses, but a major new curriculum initiative to cover 'the vital system of ideas' of the time. It is important for us to recognize that 'culture' for this writer is not 'artistic culture' but a wider concept involving scientific knowledge. It is a term closer to the German *Wissenschaft*, which in English is translated inadequately as science. In Chapter IV of *Mission of the University*, Ortega expands on what he means. The term covers the 'great cultural disciplines', namely the physical scheme of the world (physics), the fundamental themes of organic life (biology), the historical process of the human species (history), the structure and functioning of social life (sociology) and the plan of the universe (philosophy). It is easy to see why this substantial core of human learning is a radical reforming curriculum, displacing traditional courses. The existing dominance of professional training and scientific investigation or research will shrink into a lesser position if the student is to survive intellectual overload. Indeed, Ortega (like F. R. Leavis) regards the ideal university as having a centre of humane learning which permeates all its activities: 'Personally I should make a Faculty of Culture, the nucleus of the university, and of the whole of higher education' (Ortega y Gasset 1946: 68).

No-one introduces the word 'culture' into a serious discussion without a sinking feeling of imminent definition and ensuing discussion, and so I shall turn from following the main argument of *Mission of the University* to attempt an explanation of Ortega's use of the term. The previous paragraph indicates that there is a much wider meaning than the English habit of equating culture with the humanities or 'art culture'. Ortega himself is more interested in the function of culture, i.e. what it does rather than what it means. It is to see a way through 'the chaos . . . [the] tangled and confused jungle in which man is lost' (Ortega y Gasset 1946: 43). It is 'what saves human life from being a mere disaster; it is what enables man to live a life which is something above meaningless tragedy or inward disgrace', and it is 'the vital system of ideas of a period'. Whatever it contains (and as we have seen in the previous paragraph it covers a wide range of what we might now call 'disciplines'), it is the opposite of the contemporary Spanish universities' commitment. For Ortega, the university system as he knew it merely produced 'a new barbarism'.

Culture is the vital system of the period. It makes not a particle of difference whether these ideas, or convictions, lie partly or wholly in the province of science. Culture is not science. It is characteristic of our present culture that a great part of its contents proceeds out of science, but in other cultures this has not been the case, nor is it decreed anywhere that in ours it will always be so to the same degree as at present.

> Compared with the medieval university, the contemporary university has developed the mere seed of professional instruction into an enormous activity; it has added the function of research; and it has abandoned almost entirely the teaching or transmission of culture. (Ortega y Gasset 1946: 44)

'Culture', then, is to be the chief food of the student because he needs to be nourished for a future role in society, that of exerting an influence of 'diffuse pressure'. 'Diffusion' gives a clue. The aim is to educate broadly, to avoid the fragmentation of the modern specialist. The university must have the function of 'making the whole man'. (This phrase will become increasingly familiar to those who continue with the rest of this work.) Ortega then grasps the radical question which may have been prominent in the minds of those sitting at his feet in the 'teach-in'. Why do we need an institution, the university? Given that every man has the potential to be extraordinary, why risk the inhibiting nature of an institution? Here Ortega plays his first pedagogical card. Every man is not extraordinary. Teaching is necessary. Pedagogy exists because of an economic principle, the principle of shortages. All men have the capacity to learn, but a scarcity exists when this capacity is either not awakened or there is too much to learn in the time available. A primitive society does not need universities because 'there is less to learn and it is in their capacity to acquire it'. The principle of economy of learning follows from this argument of supply and demand. The content of education should relate to the capacity of the learner and to what he needs to know. The curriculum, therefore, does not rest on the nature of knowledge transferred or on the nature of the professor's knowledge about to be transferred. Pedagogic considerations steer the curriculum. 'That which is strictly necessary for the life of a man who is a student' is the first criterion. The next step is a further reduction of the curriculum of what is necessary, with the criterion for reduction being the capacity of the student to learn effectively. This is a pedagogical doctrine of parsimony. Ortega feels he is in the tradition of Goethe, with the injunction: 'Free yourself from what is superfluous to yourself' (Ortega y Gasset 1968c).

> This ascetic frugality of pretensions, this severe loyalty in recognising the limits of the attainable, will, in my belief, procure what is the university's most fundamental need: the need that its institutional life correspond squarely to its proper function and true limits, in order that its life may be genuine and sincere in its inmost dealings, I have already proposed that the

new life should take as its point of departure this simple recognition of the destiny of the individual or of the institution. All else that we may subsequently wish to make of ourselves, or of private institutions or the state, will take root and come to fruition only if we have planted its seed in the rich soil of a nature resigned to be, first of all the essential minimum which corresponds to its destiny. Europe is sick because its people profess to stand upon a precarious tenth rung in life, without having taken the trouble first to secure a footing on the elemental one, two, three. (Ortega y Gasset 1946: 74)

The final chapters of *Mission of the University* dwell on the distinction which the author must now make between culture and the type of science which is investigative or, as we would say now, research-oriented. In a typically parsimonious passage, Ortega tells us his belief that the teacher of history and a historian are different. Similarly, not all students can be scientists, nor do they need to be working on the frontiers of scientific knowledge. In fact, Ortega argues that the university does not need a continuous expansion and growth of the curriculum by research, but rather a process of systematization and synthesis of what is already known.

Readers approaching Ortega through my summary may conclude that what is presented is a reactionary doctrine, a withdrawal out of progress and a retreat into a minimalist academic programme. To counteract this view, let me recommend the final chapter of *Mission of the University*. Ortega concludes his work by taking pains to explain that the apparently ascetic and frugal presentation of the curriculum for the future has a very noble and expansive social purpose. The university, he argues, has come about in Western Europe because it signifies the European's wish to live by intellect. Science (in the form of research) must, of course, go on and indeed flourish in association with the university and the spirit of science must animate the institution. It cannot, however, dominate it. Instead, Ortega sees science research in 'camps pitched around' the universities with a continuing interrelationship between them. This separation of activities is in order to free the university so that it is open to the 'whole reality of its time'. In the social vacuum, left by the reduction of traditional powerful influences in modern times, the Press rather than the university has taken over the hearts and minds of the people (Ortega takes up this theme with greater persuasive rhetoric in *The Revolt of the Masses*). The university, he concludes, must return to its original status: 'an uplifting principle in the history of the western world' (Ortega y Gasset 1946: 78).

The main issues in the foregoing summary of *Mission of the University* are, I hope, clear. The text assumes a role for the institution, which rests on the liberal, non-materialistic belief that people change institutions and institutions can control events. The starting point – not the finishing point – of the curriculum is both the learner's 'fitting out' for future service and his or her true capacity to acquire learning. This is a pedagogic base for an institution teaching with an emphasis on process but with product clearly in mind. Above all, it is a doctrine of parsimony in learning, not the exploding university of ever-expanding knowledge, but the concentrating, synthesizing, focusing institution.

The nature of humanity: The mass and the individual

Ortega's main corpus of work confirms that this educational work was consistent with his main philosophical directions. He writes in *Mission* about humans as learners. What is his underlying belief about the nature of humanity in all their activities? We must first understand his deep antagonism to the 'masses', one antithesis of which is his belief in the special powers of some human beings. Attention to this social theory in its turn will direct our attention to Ortega's theory of the part the intellectual might play in a desirable society.

The criticism of élitism is not avoidable in Ortega's case. He clearly sees certain beings as both gifted and teachable, though he is in a peculiarly different position from traditional élite arguments. Whereas Newman had no difficulty in assuming that his readers shared his views on the continuing necessity for an already existing governing class to be educated in the best atmosphere in order to rule well, Ortega has to argue a case for creating such a class. He could not assume in contemporary Spain that the existing power-holders were the desirable class whose children had to be educated to carry on a tradition. In a chaotic political situation there was no clear certainty of any continuity for one specific élite. It is for this reason that he urgently proposes in the key work before us, as well as elsewhere, that an intellectual leader-group must be newly created. The opposition to the leader is 'mass-man', the well-known epithet from *The Revolt of the Masses*. It is not that mass-man is simply a large lumpen-proletariat. 'Mass man' may be the dominant mode within any socio-economic class. It is, as McClintock argues, a characterological not a sociological type:

> Inside each of us, two men live in a perpetual struggle, a savage man who is wilful, irreducible to a role or pattern, a species of gorilla, and a stern man who is found to be thinking exact ideas, performing legal acts, feeling emotions of transcendent values. The wild instincts exist only for the former man, the man of nature, the latter, the man of culture, alone participates in science, law and beauty'. (McClintock 1971: 28–9)

This quotation is consistent with the later thinking of Ortega. It signals too that his judgement, that action rather than contemplation is man's destiny, is an important distinction for anyone writing about the university and indispensable in considering the public role of the intellectual: 'There has to be at least a clash of action to make contemplations possible' (Ortega y Gasset 1968a: 87).

I hope enough has emerged from the previous analysis of *Mission of the University* to redress the balance or to avoid misunderstanding the last point. There is here no Nietzschian urge to act at any cost and so avoid reflection. *The Dehumanization of Art* was written at the outbreak of war in 1939 when Ortega was fully cognizant of the different strands in European political philosophy, all of which urged engagement or commitment by action. In that work, in the essay called 'The self and the other' (Ortega y Gasset 1968b), he further analyses action. There are two different states of action, the first negative and distinctive, the second leading to positive action. The former is to be 'beside oneself', a state he judges to be commonly suffered in modern society. This condition 'bemuses him, blinds him, forces him to act mechanically in a frenetic somnambulism' (Ortega y Gasset 1968b: 176). The opposite, positive state is to withdraw temporarily and then return as a protagonist to the world 'with a self he did not possess before'. The changing of the world is risky, outcomes may be totally unexpected, for nothing is given as a gift to man. 'He hopes to do it all for himself.' The university is such a place apart, a locus to think before acting. In order to earn this privilege of standing apart, the institution itself must therefore return to being a *pouvoir spirituel* in Europe.

Ortega's emphasis on the positive state of action might be presumed to lead to a doctrine of social improvement. Is humanity's power to act as a source of permanent optimism for the philosopher? The sceptical side of Ortega's nature opposes such a Utopian view. Education cannot supply tools for the successful manipulation of the world. It can equip the learner with the faculty to live authentically so that the unknown can be faced effectively. There are frequent references to the unpredictable and risky nature of life. Unlike some existential-ist writings, Ortega's view of risk is not that the exhilaration of risk is all. It is rather that action can lead someone to a still centre in the midst of uncertainty. In a remarkable passage in 'In search of Goethe from within', which contains a typical figure of speech, Ortega proposes that life is a permanent shipwreck (Ortega y Gasset 1968c). It is, however, not the sensation of being shipwrecked that excites him or the 'angst' of uncertainty, but the movement of the shipwrecked man's arms which keep him afloat. Above all else, Ortega believes in mankind's power to make himself. 'This is the vital programme.' 'Whether he be original or plagiarist, man is the novelist of himself' (Ortega y Gasset 1961: 156).

The next question must be to ask what power is it that helps the shipwrecked mariner move his arms with purpose? Ortega's answer is one of existential choice: 'To live is to feel ourselves *fatally* obliged to exercise *our liberty* to decide what we are going to be in this world' (Ortega y Gasset 1963: 36; my emphasis). Existential choice depends upon what man already knows. History is a fixed point of reliability for a journey to the future. 'Man, in a word, has no nature; what he has is . . . history' (Ortega y Gasset 1961: 157). Just as in his institutional theory the university must be modelled to be appropriate for the necessities and limitations of what the student can achieve, therefore his theory of humanity is a theory of potential based on where he starts, not on an ideal of where he should finish.

The university and the state: A doctrine of potential

The point of this excursion into the wider field of Ortega's thinking is that it puts into context the place of the mission that he established for the university. As with the institution, so with the social vision. For both university and state there is no Utopia but, at least, a conservative measure of hope. It is also important to note that it is a doctrine of potential: 'Man is a substantial emigrant on a pilgrimage of being, and it is accordingly meaningless to set limits to what he is capable of being' (Ortega y Gasset 1961: 157), yet an open unrestricted vision like this is reined back by pragmatism. Therefore, the educational doctrine of parsimony is closely related to this cautious understanding of the difficult task of the modern state. Civilized society demands subtle powers of control. The risks are high, despite the rapid advances of our time. Most important of all the achievements so far made have been based on human virtue, 'The least failure of which would cause the rapid disappearance of the whole magnificent edifice' (Ortega y Gasset 1963: 44). History, for which he held consistent respect, is at least a tool of exploration to help us reach out to understand our present society. Ideally, of course, history will encourage and inspire as well as cultivate a due wariness. In a stirring phrase in *The Revolt of the Masses*, truly 'contemporaneous' people 'feel palpitating beneath them the whole subsoil of history'. This is not a dogmatic or determinist view of the history which we might find in other contemporary ideologies. History can be ignored, but it has an awkward habit of returning: 'The past is a revenant.'

History alone is, of course, not the only tool for the 'truly contemporaneous man'. 'Wholeness' is a quality which we have already noted as a desirable feature of the educated citizen. The over-specialization of our contemporary society, encouraged by the universities, is a further example of inadequate tools for a delicate task. Ortega is in no doubt – specialization is a 'barbarism'. The well-educated leaders of the new society need much more sophisticated, thoughtful, richer devices than the ones they are currently provided with by their education. Any specific techniques they may learn there are likely to shrink in use, because, as Ortega shows in his long analysis of the change from city state to nation state in *The Revolt of the Masses*, there is nothing permanent to which those techniques can apply. The present and the future make for a new type of unfixed, ever-changing community, for the modern state is never fully formed, it is always in the process of forming. Life today 'has become scandalously provisional' (Ortega y Gasset 1963: 138). With that phrase we can readily appreciate the demanding nature of the task of those who take on the education (the higher education in every sense) of the future leaders of the ever-future state.

Ortega and our own dilemmas

It is now time to make a provisional assessment of some of the issues that Ortega left to us. He does not resolve the difficulties of reconciling open access to higher education with an educational doctrine of the formation of a leadership élite. In truth, he may be said to throw a few more tensions into the ring rather than resolving some away. His confident opinion that the power of the university is sufficient to override the power of the mass media is not easy to accept in the light of the rapidly increasing power of a wider variety of agencies of communication in the last half of the century. One is made to ask more searching political questions than Ortega does. Is it the case, for instance, that the power of the mass media resides somehow organically in the masses, or is the truth more that it lies with a small élite that controls what the masses 'need to know'? Is he, as one modern critical work asserts (Gray 1989), a 'purveyor of myths' to support critics and intellectuals in believing what they want to believe?

If these questions, so pressing in our own times, can be held in check for a time, then Ortega's value to higher education can be properly assessed. The best form of appraising that value is to concentrate on what at first sight appears to be marginal to our concerns. It is in fact the very originality and even quirkiness of the questions which he asks that makes him enter the lists of major thinkers about the purposes of higher education. Could a university or college be structured on the basis of what it is strictly necessary to learn? Is it possible that research, particularly scientific research, is a distraction from the public mission of the university rather than the commonly accepted argument that research earns the university public favour? Should scientific investigation be one of the main performance indicators as it now appears to be? Would the necessary result of answering the previous question be the establishment of research institutions around, but not in, the university? Is the 'wholeness' of the curriculum still a desirable or an achievable objective, particularly if the public mission of the university is to be the creation of the leadership of the next generation?

The central quality of 'parsimony' does deserve some consideration by those who plan the future of higher education institutions. It is true that education at all levels, schools as well as universities, are assumed by politicians and social reformers to be capable of taking on board a vast range of activities for what is deemed to be the good of their pupils and students. The range of requirements laid on teacher training institutions by government agencies in the UK (as in other countries) is formidable – knowledge of information technology, understanding language and its functions, awareness of industry, racial awareness, knowledge of gender equality, to name only a few. The time for learning and reflection on that learning is seriously reduced, so that a training course is more concerned with completing training schedules than education. Other professional courses in higher education can repeat the same prescriptive widening, the very opposite of parsimony. In many ways, the UK debate of the 1960s, about 'broad' courses as opposed to narrow courses, denied Ortega's axiom of parsimony at the same time as appearing to agree with it. It was a common theme of the 1950s and the 1960s (and the theme reappears at times in later decades) that the single-subject specialist honours degree was a process of learning too much about too little. The response was often to create variety and diversity, which in practice students themselves judged in rank order. Many responded as active, parsimonious thinkers by concentrating their efforts in one field and treating the rest of the menu as 'minor' required courses. In the event, the belief in the 'explosion of knowledge' led to the anxious response that much of the debris of the explosion must be picked up by the learner. A corresponding but different view of the explosion of knowledge is also generally held, i.e. that all learning dates quickly and it is therefore worthless to acquire it in large amounts. Strangely, this last truism about knowledge did not lead to a conservative view of the curriculum in the 1950s and 1960s, but only to a wariness about concentration. Of course, the times were expansive and developing. In the last quarter of the century with more concentrating and conservative visions of higher education, the opportunity occurs again for reviewing Ortega's dictum of doing well what can be learned well. Now is the opportunity to examine what must be learned at the beginning of a career and what can be left until experience has taught some lessons. There is life still in a doctrine of parsimony.

Many partial answers have, in short, been given in the second half of this century to questions that Ortega raised, but not because the respondents experienced the same vision as he did. New universities with novel forms of organization have been constructed to bear the weight of new curricular plans. Degree courses have been designed to cover the essentials for an educated person, but each construction appears to have been built from first principles that no-one else had ever seen. The rationale of the marketplace has been a major factor. Like Ortega, many have questioned the place of research and have tested the apparently commonsense opinion that all higher education must have a research base. However, those who have asked such questions recently have asked them in order to rationalize expensive resources. Ortega's sweep is wider than any of these piecemeal solutions, and he leaves the reader with an admiration for his ability to encompass a mission statement for higher education institutions which is both constrained by the limitations of human beings and, at the same time, ambitious for the strange, ancient institutions which, despite rapid change and pressure of circumstance, persist in Western civilization:

> It is a question of life and death for Europe to put this ridiculous situation to rights. And if this is to be done the university must intervene as the university, in current affairs, treating the great themes of the day from its own point of view: cultural, professional and scientific. Thus it will not be an institution exclusively for students, a retreat *ad usum Delphini*. In the thick of life's urgencies and its passions, the university must assert itself as a major 'spiritual power', higher than the press, standing for serenity in the midst of frenzy, for seriousness and the grasp of intellect in the face of frivolity and unashamed stupidity.
>
> Then the university, once again, will come to be what it was in its grand hour; an uplifting principle in the history of the western world. (Ortega y Gasset 1946: 77–8)

References

Gray, R. (1989). *The Imperative of Modernity: J Ortega y Gasset*. Berkeley, University of California Press.

McClintock, R. (1971). *Man and his Circumstances: Ortega as Educator*. New York, Teachers' College Press, Columbia University.

Marias, J. (1970). *José Ortega y Gasset: Circumstance and Vocation* (translated by F. M. Lopez-Morilles). Oklahoma, University of Oklahoma Press.

Moberly, W. H. (1949). *The Crisis in the University* London, S.C.M. Press.

Mora, J. Ferrater (1956). *Ortega y Gasset: An Outline of his Philosophy*. London, Bowes and Bowes.

Ortega y Gasset, J. (1946). *Mission of the University* (translated by H. L. Nostrand). London, Kegan Paul, Trench, Trubner.

Ortega y Gasset, J. (1961). 'Man has no nature'. In W. Kaufmann (Ed.), *Existentialism from Dostoevsky to Sartre*. New York, Meridian Books.

Ortega y Gasset, J. (1963). *The Revolt of the Masses*. London, Allen and Unwin.

Ortega y Gasset, J. (1968a). Notes on the novel. In *The Dehumanization of Art*. Princeton, Princeton University Press.

Ortega y Gasset, J. (1968b). The self and the other. In *The Dehumanization of Art*. Princeton, Princeton University Press.

Ortega y Gasset, J. (1968c). In search of Goethe from within. In *The Dehumanization of Art*. Princeton, Princeton University Press.

Ortega y Gasset, J. (1968d). The dehumanization of art. In *The Dehumanization of Art*. Princeton, Princeton University Press.

4

Karl Jaspers: *The Idea of the University* – Communication at the Frontiers

To turn from Ortega to Karl Jaspers is a form of delayed culture shock in itself, but a deceptive one at that. At first sight there are familiar features of the intellectual landscape, particularly the urge for wholeness, suspicion of mass society, preoccupation with culture and with the part played by history, and an attempt to map the role of the intellectual. After reading a few pages, however, the intellectual traveller realizes that the terrain is very different. Jaspers represents a massive edifice, a productive life of intense belief, carefully assembled and worked out over decades of scholarship. Compare the style of Ortega's *Mission of the University* with Jaspers' *The Idea of the University*, even through the simplifying lens of translation and you will see the major differences. Jaspers moves in an inexorable logic from first solid premises to very detailed principles. He is not without the striking phrase, but he has little of the rhetoric of Ortega. The origins of his work were, however, not only the scholar's library. They lie in the bitter feuds of the German academics before the Second World War. Just as Ortega's work was to be prophetic of crisis in the university system in Spain, so Jaspers' work not only spans the years that paved the way for European Armageddon but also arose from early experience of exclusion and persecution. That experience constructed monuments rather than decorative disquisitions.

The key text: *The Idea of the University*

Jaspers' *The Idea of the University* was published in 1947. This, in translation, is the edition we are to consider. In Germany, 24 years before, Jaspers had published a work of the same title with substantial components that he used again in 1947. He was then a comparatively young scholar working in Heidelberg. That earlier work, he tells us in an autobiographical essay (Schilpp 1957), arose from a concern for academic freedom at a time when the German universities were reassembling themselves after the defeat of the First World War and attempting to come to terms with national failure and a dangerous mood of compensatory nationalist ferment. Jaspers remembers two incidents that led him to write a text with an ambitious, forward-looking title proposing a marriage of ideals and ideas. The first was a *cause célèbre* of the time when, as a member of the university senate, he was asked to sign a petition of protest against the conditions laid upon Germany by the victorious powers. He spoke out against the petition on the grounds that the university should not engage itself in political action. Although he recognized that, like the Church, the university's existence materially depended on taxation and public support, 'Our origin lies in the European Middle Ages not in territorial states which have merely taken us over' (Schilpp 1957: 49).

The second affair that he remembered was equally typical of his thoughtful, serious consideration of the deeper implications of any public action taken by an intellectual institution. A fellow lecturer had earned himself considerable criticism and public obloquy by remarks which were interpreted as insulting to Germany's war dead. Jaspers was a member of the board of enquiry established to decide whether the offender should be expelled from his post. Jaspers tells us that he was alone in speaking against the expulsion, defending the right of freedom of speech to preserve the health of the university. Undoubtedly, in these heated times with, if they had known it, symptoms of the long serious illness soon to afflict them, Jaspers found himself opposed to the structures of power within the German universities and in particular to the strong departmental structure of the German system.

Two other biographical influences may have contributed to the 1923 version. Jaspers tells us that, as a student himself, he was suspicious of the student fraternity system which encouraged students to give up their pursuit of knowledge and of intellectual adventure in order to join a set of social privilege and character formation. In 1947, he was to reject the idea that the university was primarily constituted in order to be an institution for the training of character. His own student experience taught him that there were grave dangers of creating a conforming 'familiar type', which he quite simply hated. Equally, he disliked the notion of student life as a passage to good examination grades and career orientation. He remembers many of his own teachers as dangerously nationalist and political, not sufficiently detached from nor superior to narrow national and political concerns. In summary, they displayed 'an existential rootlessness and a confusion'. We shall see later that Jaspers had clear views on the public function of the university and the dangers of action overruling major principles of academic integrity.

Jaspers claimed that the 1923 version of *The Idea of the University* was newly written and changed in order to produce the text of 1947, although 'unchanged as to sentiment'. A brief comparison of the two texts shows more consistency even in structure than Jaspers perhaps admitted to himself, but the 1947 version is longer and, as he says in the autobiographical sketch from which I have been quoting, it was a revision to serve a particular purpose, the creation of the new German universities after 1945. If the 1923 version had emerged from a sensitive understanding of the dangers to come, the 1947 text emerges hot from the furnace of European history. That it is a logical, orderly text, methodically reviewing arguments, progressively pursuing ideas through every aspect, is a tribute to the control of a writer who had suffered extreme indignity in the intervening years.

For Jaspers, 1923–31 was 'a period of public silence', occupied with teaching and preparation but not publication. From 1931, he began to produce major works, but increasingly came under political attack for his outspoken views on academic freedom and for his undisguised opposition to the obscurantism of National Socialism, which steadily infiltrated the university system. In 1937, he was deprived of his professorship and in 1938 he was forbidden to publish. Throughout the war, unable to teach or to write, he lived in limited freedom, but not without fear. This was a period of intense study, diversifying his interests from philosophy and psychoanalysis into sociology and theology. In 1945, when the Allied forces entered Heidelberg, his name and that of his wife were found in lists of those about to be sent to concentration camps. The war ended just in time for them, and almost immediately Jaspers became involved in active academic business. He was reinstated as a professor and began to work for the reconstruction of the German university system. *Der Idee der Universität* was therefore written at a critical moment of re-birth, plunging into the field of controversy without delay. Simultaneously, Jaspers was practically involved. Very quickly his book achieved some of its aims in the formation of new university structures.

The English version of *Der Idee* was published in London in 1960. The translation omits about eight pages of the original which the editor considered to be relevant only to the West German position in 1947. The timing of the English publication was important. It emerged during the period in the UK when the Robbins Committee was engaged on its deliberations. We cannot know if there was any direct influence on the committee. In terms of press reviews, it must have been a disappointment to its publisher and editor. The longest review I can trace is in *The Universities Quarterly* (Wilcher 1960), where it was paired with the autobiographical musings of an Australian vice-chancellor, with rather more warm attention to the latter. It was cautiously and briefly commented on in a few lines in one or two other journals, receiving only one major review of approval, from Eric Ashby (1960) in *The New Statesman*. Ashby had the perception to see that it was a profound work of more significance than its style (judged to be weightily teutonic) might suggest. As for the rest of the reviewers, it was nervously discussed in a few lines as a document of conservatism at a time when academic commentators of all kinds were urging the need for radical change in the UK's higher educational scene. I shall now attempt a summary of the text, leaving a detailed analysis of major themes until the whole carefully articulated plan has been set out.

The book begins with a classic statement: 'The University is a community of scholars and students engaged in the task of seeking truth.' The institution in a sense needs no further legitimation because a place to seek truth is a human right, but there is a heavy responsibility attached to this right. Freedom to teach truth lays upon the university the obligation to do so in defiance of anyone inside or outside the institution who tries to curtail truth. The search for truth is more important than other apparently practical purposes of the institution. Jaspers then explores the human desire to seek truth, explaining it in a typically existentialist way as a quest for wholeness. This affirmation takes him in turn to an examination of the nature of science and of the intellectual life as a whole. A basic distinction between 'narrow science', 'wider science' and philosophy is made, and the proposition that scientific knowledge can only lead to provisional and partial knowledge of the whole is established. Having described the ideal type of scientific and scholarly discipline, he considered the special area of the transmission of culture, which is one of the three commonly ascribed functions of a university alongside research and the transmission of learning for professional training and education.

The next section of the book on pedagogical matters is virtually unaltered from the 1923 edition, where there was a similar historical analysis of what Jaspers saw as the main methods of learning and teaching: by scholastic methods, by apprenticeship systems and by Socratic dialogue. He typically argues in favour of a style of teaching which is grounded on faith in the value of the search for wholeness and therefore for truth. A developed form of the Socratic system appeals to him because it does not take place in isolation: 'University education is a formative process arriving at meaningful freedom. It takes place through participation in the university's intellectual life' (Jaspers 1960: 65).

Perhaps the pivotal part of the book and of his argument is the section on communication, which, as I shall explain later, is a major concept in Jaspers' argument for the value of an institution. It is also basic to our understanding of an existentialist grasping the nettle of institutional value. At this point, let it suffice to summarize the main point that communication in 'a community of thinking' is directly related to the quintessential feature of the ideal university, namely the freedom of intellect. Jaspers then takes up practical reasons for the existence of universities, which are the Western world's demonstration of what he calls the Western supernatural idea, of Graeco-German origin. The university is, in short, 'the locus of this ideal'. The common question which taxes most thinkers on higher education is next tackled: 'What is to be included in the curriculum?' Jaspers is generous in his inclusions. He tries to avoid polarities such as practical and theoretical classifications of knowledge. Instead, he chooses what he calls a concentric view of two groups or series of subjects – one including physics, chemistry, psychology and sociology, which 'seek the universal', and the other including history, 'concerning the individual and the unique'. Technology is to be admitted in order that it can be humanized and infused with meaning and purpose. Jaspers' mission for wholeness necessarily leads him to a comprehensiveness of knowledge.

The quality of the institution is less defined by what it teaches than by who teaches and how they teach. Overall, the energy driving the university comes from a belief in the infinite possibility of human nature: 'The whole courage to educate derives from a trust in such dormant possibilities' (Jaspers 1960: 117). This potential for human development is (or rather ought to be) of central concern to the state. The university must be free because it acts as an intellectual conscience to the state. As such it is not a political tool but, because it speaks from a basis of knowledge, it can fundamentally affect action: 'It controls the state through the power of truth not of force' (Jaspers 1960: 135). Not surprisingly, Jaspers is then led to face the fact that, although all men have a dormant possibility, few are selected, by fortune or by chance, to undergo the awakening process for which the ideal university exists. An intellectual aristocracy is not something to be avoided, but rather one to be encouraged, because it will represent the immense possibility of mankind. Put simply, this élite will earn the most precious human acquisition: they will know themselves and thence the world will know them as bearers of 'man's humanity *par excellence*'. They must be doubly sure that they are not politically partial, remaining faithful to the pursuit of the truth. So Jaspers returns in the end to his starting point: the university has a privilege of independent existence earned by accepting the obligation to teach truth.

The difficulty with Jaspers, despite the apparently linear argument of any particular section, is breaking into the logical sequence of thought in order to carry out an examination of one thread. This is as true in terms of the chronology of Jaspers' corpus as it is within any one text written in a defined period. Jaspers' early work can be put alongside later major pieces and we see the same conviction at work, only filled out and made more wide-reaching in cultural scope by the advance of his own encyclopaedic studies. Wherever we take as a starting point, it leads us to the vision of humanity and its risky potential; therefore, rather than extracting his theory of learning and working on to his doctrine of humanity, let us do the opposite and see first what kind of view of humanity he holds and then examine his view of how learning is appropriate to that vision.

Karl Jaspers' conception of humanity

The Idea of the University provides in its own pages enough instances of Jaspers' concept of the nature of human beings, almost without recourse to more famous major texts. Here are a number of quotations from *The Idea of the University* to illustrate Jaspers' conception of Man as a potential being in a complex condition of limitation and capability. They provide a framework for us to fill in the picture from wider sources of reading. All these features or aspects of the Jaspers' person lead in the key text in question to a definition of the learner:

1. Humanity is potentially free: 'Man is the source of all his own decisions. That I am made that way is only a device for evading freedom' (Jaspers 1960: 116).
2. Despite the gift of freedom, human beings exist within limitations and constraints both by the very nature of their physical existence, suffering and death, and by the social structures they create: 'It is up to each man to accept his limitations and to achieve freedom within them' (Jaspers 1960: 119).
3. The search for freedom despite limitation is a search for wholeness and for something beyond oneself which is itself whole and complete. That search is the first step to knowledge: 'Oneness and wholeness are the very essence of man's will to know' (Jaspers 1960: 20).

4. A person is a creature distinguished by a will to know the truth, a will to learn: 'Man alone among other beings considers himself in the process of knowledge' (Jaspers 1960: 32). 'The University demands a ruthless will to know' (ibid.: 66).

5. The tension between the human capability and actuality, between his or her sense of individuality and his or her sense of belonging to humanity, between what one's faculties allow one to know and what there is to know is a creative tension out of which awareness growth and self-identity arise: 'Its (the university's) principle is to furnish all the tools and offer all possibilities in the province of the intellect, to direct the individual to the frontiers, to refer the learner back to himself for all his decisions, to his own sense of responsibility' (Jaspers 1960: 66).

This list is enough indication of a philosophy of human nature to indicate how different Jaspers is from other contemporaries and their views of man's estate. The following paragraphs select one or two themes from this rounded complex of theses and antitheses, of possibility and limitation. These themes concentrate on the human being as a learner and the institution that can best enable learning.

Learning as the quest for transcendence

In answer to the questions 'Why does man learn?' and 'What is the source of his drive for knowledge?', Jaspers consistently refers back to his conception of human beings as seeking something other than their present bounded state. In *Truth and Symbol*, he proposes that 'astonishment' is the source of learning even at an advanced level: 'Philosophy begins with astonishment. Astonishment turns into questioning' (Jaspers 1959: 70). At one time, he talks of 'determination', at others, of 'will'. Again, he refers to 'a serious and unconditional commitment to a search for transcendence'. The quest for wholeness is almost described in terms of instinct or drive. We shall see later that Jaspers is under no Romantic illusion that all are natural hunters after the elusive prey of knowledge. Mass society can reduce or condition human beings to a state of apathy. What distinguishes the university in its singleness of purpose is that it stands back from the mass of society and enables its members to satisfy, in a uniquely privileged situation, a human drive, a form of fulfilment within the limitations of any human activity. It is with 'limitation' and 'boundary' that we can begin to examine the distinctive features of the human learner. The constraints in their turn determine the ideal university.

Tension and limitation

Wallraff (1970: 142) says that Jaspers' explication of severance (*die Trennung*), or the opposing tension between opposing forces, was one of his special contributions to the existentialist movement. Dysfunction or severance can be disabling and intellectually depressing, but in Jaspers' terminology, *die Trennung* is potentially a positive force for intellectual progress and in itself a source of cognition. It is possible to distinguish at least three ways in which humanity as learners are pulled in opposing directions. The intellectual is both inside the world and, on the contrary, standing against it (Olsen 1979). As early as 1931, in *Man in the Modern Age*, Jaspers writes: 'Selfhood or self-existence first arises out of his being against the world in the world.' Note here that this type of tension is essentially a state of self-awareness. The second kind of tension is in the traditional divide between contemplation and action. The intellectual can see the opposition of 'technical mass order' (as Jaspers puts it in *Man in the Modern Age*) and full human life. His message to the intellectual is as important to the university as it is to the individual, for it is in the university that the learner steps temporarily out of action before returning to play an active part in the world:

> Thus we have to live, as it were, upon a narrow mountain ridge, falling away on one side into the mere enterprise or, on the other, into a life devoid of reality, side by side with the enterprise. (Jaspers 1951: 179)

Finally, there is the tension integral to any search for truth, between what you want to know and the limitation of what can be known. Human reason founders on limitations, some small and physical, some large and super-human, such as death, suffering and conflict. Reason takes us then to a boundary situation (*Grenzensituationen* in *Truth and Symbol*, Jaspers 1959), but that boundary must be seen as a beckoning challenge to enter a new world over the horizon rather than a forbidding 'no-go' sign, the impossible terminus of enquiry. In Jaspers' later works, he seeks in *Grenzensituationen* the 'cyphers' or signs by which a person can reach into new territories of understanding. Such a reaching out becomes a key moment of transcendence when the full potential of Humanity can be achieved. Reason is essential, as it were, for the forced march to the frontier, but beyond it there are signs to read in a language other than reason provides. 'The glimmer of ambiguous symbols', as he describes this extra-rational position, is not alien to the university. Indeed, an acknowledgement of this language of symbols or cyphers reinforces Jaspers' own views on the need for a catholic portfolio of courses in the university. Reason-led-sciences (in the broadest sense of *Wissenschaft*) are partners with other kinds of intellectual activity, not the least of which is philosophy. The product of the university is encouraged to be receptive to this glimmer beyond the limits of reason, for the university's task is to develop the power of 'responsive reason' in its alumni.

I have concentrated on Jaspers' analysis of dysfunction, tension or *die Trennung* because it amply demonstrates three of his most striking features as a thinker about the role of the intellectual and hence the shape of the ideal university. Tension is itself a source of cognition. Tension awakens by astonishing the receptive student and in boundary situations that student becomes self-aware, an essential step towards transcending the self. Finally, at points of tension, the intellectual has to deploy a range of intellectual activities, a full range of which the university must admit within its own frontiers. Indeed, to move to the next main feature of Jaspers' intellectual map, it is essential that the sciences, the arts and philosophy do not only relate to and communicate with one another all the way towards this fruitful frontier, but also beyond it.

The university and the essential nature of communication

Open communication is an essential value not only at the core of Jaspers' intellectual scheme, but also at the heart of his justification of the liberal university. The historical background of his life as a university teacher goes some way to explain his preoccupation with this essential feature of good learning. The German universities between the wars can be readily criticized for having failed good standards of communication in at least three ways. First, and most seriously, many of Jaspers' colleagues had bowed to force under Hitler's regime and, bending the search for truth, perverted their powerful base as communicators to the young. Secondly, tyranny had stopped communication effectively by banning writing and teaching. Thirdly there was the longstanding, strongly separated structures of the German university departmental system. The professorially dominated subject structures stood as living examples of divisions rather than of wholeness, the contradiction of communication and collaboration across boundaries.

Of course, Jaspers' insistence on the value of communication does not only rest on his own personal history. It lies bedded in his world-view of the importance of wholeness and the diminishing nature of partial insights. Carr (1974) illustrates this point well from Jaspers' *Psychologisch Weltanschauungen* as early as 1919. We have already seen that in subsequent writing, there is continuous attention to *Grenzensituationen*, but, more to this particular point, that concept has a correlate in the theme of communication. An awareness of boundaries and limitations can create despair, but speaking to others is a way out of that despair. We all experience the same terrifying aspects of lack of wholeness – guilt, suffering, death. Conversely, we also all have the possibility of individual freedom, but that freedom again is only possible because others can share in it with us. In Jaspers' major work on philosophy, there is a typical three-fold definition of communication (see Jaspers 1969): (1) the naive, unproblematic exchange between people; (2) the deeper exchange between egos which have learned to distinguish themselves carefully from their fellows, and from the world around them; and (3), the most significant for our present study, the communication of a sense of community through a shared idea of totality. In respect of this third type, Jaspers instances specifically a state, a profession or a university. Obviously, the initial establishment of an institution is not enough. Its original momentum may not last. What counts, as always, is the quality of the individuals in the organization who, through one means or another (and philosophy is put forward as the chief means at this point), come to 'a form of thinking which constantly strives to connect the various modes to form a totality'. Philosophy does not act only within the individual and inside his or her portfolio of knowledge. It operates between individuals with all their differences. Hamilton (1976) has pointed out that philosophy, for Jaspers as for other thinkers, is not a lonely art but one accomplished by meeting and communicating.

We would be wrong, however, to assume that because Jaspers is saying 'only communicate' to us, his intention is to create consensus. The importance of recognizing communication in the university is not because Jaspers believes in uniformity for its own sake. He is clear that there are genuine basic differences between different forms of knowledge. Jaspers spends a considerable amount of effort both in *The Idea of the University* and in *Truth and Symbol* distinguishing between science, philosophy and history. Meeting others in the university may well lead to recognition not of unity but of differences between forms of knowledge. The scholar, unless he or she works alone, is constantly communicating across boundary/severance situations. Such communication is fruitful and educative but not inevitably reconciling, yet reconciliation is not the aim and purpose of the university. Knowing the differences between different forms of study helps each scholar to know himself or herself better. By communication with others in the ideal university, the awakened, self-aware student completes the process of education in a sharing in the human condition. In the ideal university, then, goals for the future, on this basis of truth about others and oneself, are more firmly established. The planning of courses and programmes of study and other practical activities can then take place on a basis of true knowledge.

The university and its public role: The limitations and enslavement of society

The limitations of man's potential have already received attention above in an intellectual sense, but there is good reason for attending to the social conditioning of the self and to the limitations imposed by man in society. The long study called *Man in the Modern Age*, although it has a message of hope, is not at heart a cheerful book to read. Written in 1931, it was prophetic of the power of the modern state with its ability to transform 'human beings into the functions of a titanic apparatus' (Jaspers 1951: 203). Like Ortega y Gasset, Jaspers is deeply critical of mankind in a state of mass rule, but he is perhaps even more conscious than Ortega of the all-too-easy enslavement of the mind and the denial of human possibility. In this work and in *The Origin and Goal of History*, which also takes up the theme of the decline in the richness and the possibility of life, we see Jaspers at his most conservative and yet, at the same time, in individual terms, his most hopeful. The later work is, if anything, more sombre in its forecast of the effect of the titanic apparatus of the state. Written in 1949, after he had absorbed and meditated on the destruction and reconstruction of German society, Jaspers wrote of 'the period of catastrophic descent into poverty of spirit, of humanity, love and creature energy' (Jaspers 1953: 97). In 1931, Jaspers set out his own logic of the two ways by which man could break out of the trap of modern life which led him and others like him into a state of pessimism: 'In so far as conscious will has anything to do with the matter, our future entirely depends upon political and educational activity' (Jaspers 1951: 85). Political action or the actions of the state leave him sceptical. Education is not seized on as an easy antidote. At least in Jaspers' view it offers the possibility of a route for the few to find themselves. His arguments for a qualified ray of hope in education are summarized in the following paragraphs.

In the first place, Jaspers is cautious about the effectiveness of education. We may seriously overestimate its power. The 'culture' of modern man is acquired from a variety of sources, only one of which is formal education. In more stable societies of the past, education had a self-evident value so that the educator was self-consciously 'surviving in the stream of mankind in the making', but, in rapidly changing times, education itself becomes insecure, questionable and shows symptoms of disintegration. He vividly describes the all-too present modern panic of educators, some of whom look back for old certainties, others concentrate on narrow training for skills, others yet again will pursue constant experimentation. He notes that the nation as a whole may turn its attention anxiously to education, for a solution to extraneous all-pervading problems: 'An epoch which does not trust its own self is anxiously concerned about education as if in this domain something could once more be made out of Nothingness' (Jaspers 1951: 105).

All sorts of dreams are pursued, such as the cult and veneration of youth, all indicating the forlorness of mankind. Jaspers, in short, doubts the power of education to transform society. He is even more distrustful of how the state may react if it sees education as a social engineer of learning. At best, it may decide to protect an educational system, including the university. At worst, it may take an active step and try to shape the system, to impose a malformed character-making policy on people. This last step is doomed to failure, but in the process of application, the policy will destroy both the search for truth and the institutions that attempt to pursue truth.

What then resides in education, and in particular in the university which can give hope for its own future and for the future of the civilized world? By 1949, Jaspers is clear that justification for the continuation of the university can only rest on a spiritual concern lying at the heart of an educational system; that is to say, a concern and *raison d'être* relying on a spiritual confidence, not on an economic or material or even a social justification. Character formation is not, he argues, the prime objective of the university, although it may arise as a secondary result of good teaching. In the final analysis, the aim of the university must be to train the inner being, a form of training attainable only by a few (Jaspers 1951: 108–109). Here is an unequivocal statement of a selective, élite educational philosophy. We shall see later how he justifies that selection of excellence so that there is an eventual benefit for society as a whole.

Jaspers' political philosophy, at least in respect of education, is thus individualistic, in favour of personal solutions rather than based on imposed social engineering. He is suspicious of mass schemes of human renewal. In a selection of essays and lectures translated into English as *Philosophy and the World* (Jaspers 1963), there is a typically conservative title to one section: 'The limits of educational planning'. In this passage, he examines a variety of common definitions of worthwhile education such as 'Teaching children skills and knowledge', 'Children should be educated according to aptitudes and abilities', 'Schools should turn children into useful members of the community'. None of these nostrums is wrong in itself, but overemphasis and consequent creation of institutional structures based on any one of them can move a free society closer to totalitarianism. What disappears in an urgent quest for vocational or social ends is education's 'integral tradition, the belief in a spiritual community' (Jaspers 1963: 28). In a quotation typical of nineteenth-century liberalism, Jaspers sums up his own view that the philosopher's advice is 'planning for not planning'. In the last analysis (and perhaps even from the first), 'What counts is done by the individual teacher between the four walls of his classroom where he is free and on his own' (Jaspers 1963: 31). This individuality is then qualified by the school's organization, which organization should be at a minimum. Much of this argument about teaching young children applies to the university. In his *Philosophical Autobiography* of 1957, Jaspers sums up his own experience of university teaching in a very similar manner: 'The idea of the university lives decisively in the individual students and professors and only secondarily in the forms of the institution' (Schilpp 1957: 52).

How should we teach and what should be taught?

What does Jaspers have to say about pedagogics? What in fact should be the principle on which the individualist bases his teaching of groups? Of prime importance, not surprisingly in the light of his emphasis on communication, is dialogue with other minds, particularly those in the great humanistic tradition of the West. The teacher must ensure access to this well-spring of 'What in the West, makes man all that he can be?' (Jaspers 1951: 116). In the same text, Jaspers seems to say that it is possible to be 'in touch' with this source even without teachers, but he is also clear that, in practice, fewer and fewer can, by themselves, achieve full education. Dialogue should be the prime 'method' of the university teacher. As we have noted, Jaspers has a firm commitment to the Socratic method. He expresses a preference in teaching at this level not for a formal curriculum consisting of a set body of facts, but a location where the relationship between good teachers and students can be deployed.

The Socratic method has obvious appeal to him because it rests on the innate possibilities of man. The dialogue between teacher and student tests the inner life. To Jaspers, immersed for a long period in a study of psychoanalysis, the method itself leads to an awakening, fulfilling his chief objective of teaching a student through the twin visions, knowledge of self and knowledge of the boundaries of life outside self. The good educator must always be conscious of the independent existence of the student. There is danger in any drift towards treating the learner as a machine. Attempts that have been made to engineer and mould learning have always ended in failure and rebellion. As we have already seen in this chapter, learning can change people for good or for evil. The true teacher has to acknowledge the unknown and unknowable effects of the learning process and this acknowledgement should lead to a mixture of open scepticism as a balance against the hope that energizes his professional will: 'One of his [Man's] essential traits is to be changed by his cognition in incalculable ways' (Jaspers 1963: 148).

Finally, in this section, we should pause to look at the implications for the curriculum of a university. I have already indicated in the summary of the key text that Jaspers holds a policy of catholic admission. Some aspects of his attitudes to the disciplines in a university's prospectus are worth attention. They can be found in a variety of his work, not only in *The Idea of the University*. In general, his views rely again on the concepts of limitation and its transcendence into the unknown by scholarship. As with Ortega y Gasset, we have a curricular policy of parsimony, but for different reasons. Ortega is basically cautious of Man's ability to grasp a wide range of academic experiences. Jaspers is suspicious of the capacity of the discipline not of the disciple.

In case there is any presumption that Jaspers spoke partially, that is to say only from the point of view of the humanities, it should be clearly emphasized that he writes with encouragement about scientific study. He understood the significance for the university of physical and biological sciences. In the *Origin and Goal of History*, he considers that, although the Modern Age is not an 'axial age', it is distinguished by the rapid development of both science and technology. This text (which incidentally in this respect almost exactly repeats *The Idea of the University*), admits the power and intellectual respectability of these academic studies, with one caveat, which is that 'true science' is conscious of its own limits. 'False science' has a belief in the perfectibility of the world through scientific knowledge.

It is the disciplinary processes of science that appeal to Jaspers. The three scientific functions of cognition, cogency and universal validity are all appropriate techniques to deploy in other fields of learning. The error is to believe that these techniques can teach a student everything there is to know. Science tells us what it does not know, just as it tells us with qualified certainty what it can help the student to know. Science, like reason, is limited but of essential value up to a point, and that point is valuable, when a further quality of mind is needed. *Vernunft* (common human reason or judgement) is a wider good at which Jaspers wishes us to aim. Philosophy is the key discipline or subject to help the student move those extra steps of understanding which science cannot take. Both are indispensable to each other. Wallraff (1970) sets out the close relationship in some detail. He clearly summarizes the differences and dependencies thus:

1. 'They are not the same. It is confusing to believe that the knowledge Man can prove is the same as the convictions by which he lives' (Wallraff 1970: 63).

2. Philosophy relies on science for knowledge which is uniquely reliable.
3. The results of science are by definition open to evaluation and that process reveals the limitations of what is being claimed. These limitations in turn display the areas open to philosophic investigation.
4. Arising from this partnership is the paradox that rational science discloses both the rationality and the irrationality of our world.

A short comment on another important but controversial subject is required. Jaspers is not the thinker to neglect the debates of the mid-century. He engages in *Man in the Modern Age* and inevitably in *The Origin and Goal of History* with the major critical point of the importance (or lack of it) of history. As any individualistic thinker, he is wary of theories which assert that history determines individual fate. He keeps his contemporaries' obsession with the looming domination of history at arms' length. Just as Ortega sees history as a springboard, so Jaspers interprets humanity as capable of springing free of its past, if the will is there to do so. Jaspers sees history as a channel of pedagogic importance. He seems to say to us that the engagement of the student with minds of the past is an essential process of communication. The important point, however, is that history does not lead, it is kept in its place.

The legitimization of an institution

All the arguments advanced so far through Jaspers' key text on the idea of the university and his major works which so consistently support it are arguments of individual self-knowledge and development. How does Jaspers justify an institution like a university in the face of the strongly personal salvation that he advances as the main point of the educative process? This is an area of some concern to writers of and about existentialism. It is a school of thought usually strongly critical of, or at least wary of, the power of institutions. Many followers see institutions restraining life and freedom by creating modes of 'inauthentic being'. If existentialist writings are prepared to say a lot about institutional morality, whether that is found in the Church, the state or some other engine of non-being, they have usually little to say about institutional formation. We have already seen that Jaspers held to a liberal view that less planning was preferable to more, and that he was deeply critical of attempts to create schools which aimed to change their pupils into products of a prearranged system. Unlike Cardinal Newman's *Idea*, Jaspers' *Idea of the University* is opposed to the argument that the major function of the university is the shaping of the youthful character. Nevertheless, despite all these predictable signs of anti-institutionalism, Jaspers has a strong sense of the importance of the university as an organization which can enable true learning to be achieved. It is important to realize that his educational doctrine of individual self-fulfilment and personal self-awareness has, in parallel as it were, a deeply important social fulfilment and social purpose.

Jaspers' view of the university is to provide a place of withdrawal from the world before a return to public life. This is not to say that the scholar is likely to be free from social action. His own experiences did not lead him to withdraw from public action; on the contrary, he became a contentious, outspoken figure whenever he was permitted to be so. He is, however, sure that the university acting as a unity or as a representation of learning must act in a different way than the individuals within it are impelled to act by circumstance or conscience. His view of the university as an institution standing back from direct engagement is powerful in his early pronouncements and even stronger after his experience of totalitarian rule. He consistently held the view that direct engagement of the university leads only to the perversion of truth. Typically, he applies irresistible logic which led him to equate the value of communication, on which both he and we have spent some time, as primarily a value based on the free and open sharing of views, wherever they began or wherever they led. A university that attempted to pursue a political message or doctrine would, in his view, rapidly end by limiting the freedom of the participants to engage in this essential task of open-ended communication. The purpose of the dialogue that goes on in a university, however, is in no doubt. That purpose is to influence society by the undoubted force of its struggle with truth. The university is thus to be a critical force in society, if not a direct force of intervention.

The form of the university, or its internal structures is, in Jaspers' view, related to its moral and social purpose. In *The Idea of the University*, Jaspers spends some time reflecting on his experience of the dangers of departmentalism. The strength of the university lies in the points of contact between departments, not in the concentration in a discipline. The catholicity of the university's range of subjects is of fundamental importance for truth. Jaspers doubts the wisdom of separated research institutes, a feature of higher education in Germany over a substantial period (to be explored further in Chapter 5). The broader the range of intellectual activity in a university, the stronger the safeguards against partiality. Communication across many divides is, as we have seen, at the very heart of Jaspers' argument. It is also an essential element of academic freedom. No one discipline should command the community of scholars, because such a leadership might be an implicit denial of wholeness and thence a curtailment of truth. However, philosophy has a binding, unifying function, and therefore should hold a key place in the curriculum. The university's structure should, in short, reflect a democracy of equals.

The *Idea of the University* sees the objectives of the university as three-fold: *research*, the transmission of *learning* and the transmission of *culture*. All three are part of the whole and should not be considered in isolation. As will be obvious from the last paragraph, research should not be separated from the universality of the institution by hiving off into separate institutions. The research scholar's links with the totality of the university's range of disciplines are two-fold. First, is the range of his or her studies: 'Whatever exists in the world should be brought into the scope of the university so as to become the object for study' (Jaspers 1960: 56). Second, the researcher gains by belonging to an institution with a range of interests in which he or she can carry on a 'living exchange with the scholarly community to which some day he may return' (Jaspers 1960: 57).

Jaspers, in common with other European thinkers of his day, placed great emphasis on the role of the university in educating the professionals (or, as he calls them, 'the intellectual professions'), i.e. doctor, teacher, administrator, lawyer, clergyman and architect. These professions are to do with the condition of human life as a whole. The university is therefore the appropriate place for them. In British writing on higher education, compared with European sources, there is less emphasis or rather less precision of concern about the university's function in creating a professional sector of society. The *Bildung* tradition in Germany, with its deep-rooted view of the effect of culture on social leadership and character training, particularly of the civil service and military professions, remains distinctive and active in the literature. Jaspers does not reject this tradition, but he modifies its optimism. The university is, at best, likely to create an 'active intelligence' in its ideal students, but the type of personality is produced as a 'spontaneous by-product not a conscious goal'. If we establish 'personality' as a goal in itself isolated from scholarship, then we lose intellectual integrity. Furthermore, we should not confuse the university's function with preparation for leadership in society. The professional is only a leader in the limited sense of the expertise he has gained and the formal authority granted to him by society. Leadership of society is a wider issue than the university can or should encompass. Leaders come from all classes and occupations, their expertise arises from a wider range of experience and the personal qualities demanded are not necessarily intellectual ones, but issues of will power, deliberation and an eye for reality. Thus, in the process of considering the purpose of the university, we should not confuse the aims of true learning with extraneous targets which the university is not fitted to achieve. The university's aim is for a distinctive quality of mind, at various places in Jaspers' work described as 'responsive reason', 'an active intelligence', 'the rational and philosophical influence'. There is no doubt in Jaspers' mind such qualities will be of great value in the world outside the university.

In summary, then, the institution is justified because it directs its attention to a particular form of human understanding, a distinctive quality of mind. Although this way of knowing is not the only way to help people to transcend the life they have inherited, it is a uniquely valuable way of life, particularly for those in the culture of Western Europe. There will be specific moments of trial for an institution when it must test whether it is running on track with this overall objective. Such moments are, for example, when a decision has to be made about the admission of a new discipline or area of study. Jaspers proposes criteria for such an admission. The newly proposed discipline applying for entry to the university must demonstrate an awareness of what he calls the 'basic sciences', and certify that the professors are conscious of the hierarchy of basic and auxiliary sciences. By this term 'basic science', he means, for example, a wide range of intellectual attitudes of a logical method, of cogent analysis of evidence and of an aim to be universally valid. 'Narrow science', as he calls it early in *The Idea of the University*, is limited to the study of appearances, and it is this limited study that falls to a low place in the hierarchy of sciences. So, in the admission to the university of a new discipline, Jaspers would seek for potential in the new area of knowledge and look for a demonstration that it can 'develop into an integral whole in touch with universal ideas and so remain a basic science' (Jaspers 1960: 102). This test of legitimacy of a subject discipline is, at heart, the same as the test for the legitimacy of the university as a whole – that is to say, it is justified in terms of its own high standards of scholarly activity.

Finally, we must ask (as any politician would also ask) 'How can a self-regulating and self-legitimating institution be justified in a modern state', or to use modern terminology, 'How is it accountable?' We have seen already that Jasper warns the university from the bitterness of his own experience about the dangers of direct participation in political events. In the ninth chapter of *The Idea of the University*, Jaspers deals with the relationship of state and university in the following logical manner. The university is given freedom to act, which is made possible by the state. In return, it acts as the state's 'intellectual conscience'. The university's power is solely intellectual. It is this power 'which must compel the public mind to clarify its thinking and discern its proper objectives' (Jaspers 1960: 135). The ideal example, not surprisingly, is Socrates, who probed the state with questions. A second argument arises in parallel to justify the state's support and non-interference. It is that the university has the social role of improving humanity: 'Seeking truth and the improvement of mankind, the university aims to stand for man's humanity "par excellence"' (Jaspers 1960: 145).

On these idealistic notes, we should end this study of what Jaspers has said and briefly consider what he means to us today.

The continuing values of Jaspers' thinking

At first sight, much of Jaspers' thinking about the university seems to be strangely distant from our own preoccupations. I doubt if he engages at any point with such hotly debated issues as student grants, public funding, inter-institutional competition and the age participation rate. What he writes about, however, is a perennial and deep topic, and it is vital that we now engage, as Jaspers himself would argue, in communication with a great mind.

The issue of academic freedom, and to Jaspers its inextricable relationship with the quest for truth, will always be with us. Perhaps at times when freedom is not being debated it is most at risk. Jaspers' passionate argument in favour of academic freedom is, however, as much an argument for the freedom of the individual in any walk of society as it is about the individual in a limited academic context. Indeed, the state which burns books or prescribes what can and cannot be taught does not contain its inhibiting behaviour to the world within the university's doors. The critical role of the university is one way of safeguarding the freedom of the whole community, although it must not consider itself the only way.

An evaluation of Jaspers' enthusiasm for freedom must be coloured by what I have described as his conservatism. In the first place, he is conservative about the capacity of education, in school or college, to change the world. We shall find throughout all his readings an optimism but not a utopianism. The issue of selective membership of the university has to be grasped. Jaspers is clear about the nature of this process. Not all can be selected to benefit by the life of the mind. He compensates this remark by disclaiming, as we have seen, that the university's function is to train a leadership core. There are other routes to fulfilment other than formal education, but for those who have the intellectual activity, married to energy and will, there is a considerable self-justifying reward in learning. Brubacher (1977) calls the Jaspers' élite a 'Jeffersonian' élite, rather than an aristocratic one, selection being by ability. The price to be paid, however, is a commitment to the rest of mankind. Small wonder that Jaspers himself refers to this special group of people as a 'nobility'. Small wonder too that his ideas have met with opposition in the second half of this outwardly democratic century.

The most important intellectual gift he has to leave with us is his solid, patiently argued encouragement for the life of the intellect itself. His staunch arguments for intellectual pursuits as ways of authenticity are a counterbalance to relativism and to scepticism about the processes of learning that have tended to dominate the last 40 years of the century (if not the last 100 years). These arguments are remarkably consistent in book after book throughout his lifetime. As Wallraff (1970) says, cognition and freedom are related for him, since without knowledge there is no choice and therefore no real freedom. We have seen that Jaspers sets the boundaries for the distance reason can travel, but he is never in any doubt that the journey begins with reason. The goals of learning may change because the thinker changes as the act of cognition takes place, but intellectual activity moves the person on. Of course, Jaspers' value to us is not merely to justify the line of reason and to oppose forces of un-reason that threatened to engulf Europe. He proposed a much more subtle response, in the form of full academic life. The 'responsive scholar' is able to comprehend the world, assisted by his or her acquisition of a wide range of cultivated faculties. This ideal scholar also broadens the base of the institution in which he or she studies and enriches the society which that institution serves. Furthermore, we inherit from Jaspers, if we wish to take up what he has left us, an open view of learning. Whereas in recent years, many have sought security by prescribing curricula in national plans or proscriptive forms of accreditation, the university is still, thank heaven, a place where the pursuit of knowledge can lead to unexpected conclusions and lateral connections with other disciplines. The truth served by the university is not a contained and finite truth, but an ever-open unrolling horizon.

The final point on which at this stage we should leave Jaspers, is to repeat again the essentially hopeful nature of his work. He is significant for the late twentieth century because he turns towards the traditional Western institution, the university, as a place of freedom rather than turning his back on it. We have already remarked on his positive belief in the value of the organization, despite his clear commitment to existentialism, a movement not renowned for a trust in social structures. Of course, this trust rests on a belief that such institutions can be arranged to enable people to develop to very high levels of human achievement. Niblett, in a seminal essay, making interesting comparisons between Jaspers and Marcel, comments: 'Their stress is upon the need for educating the person, not only the functionary' (Niblett 1964: 110).

This quotation usefully summarizes the pervading aspect of Jaspers' work, his essential belief and trust in what people can become. It is Jaspers' special gift to articulate not just the spirit of his time which he would have regarded as fit praise for an inspired thinker, but also to articulate the most humane and hopeful aspect of the future landscape of humanity, when such optimism was (and perhaps still is) surrounded by dark clouds and encroaching wilderness. The university as an instrument of awareness is like a flare which illuminates the landscape and the inhabitants within it.

References

Ashby, E. (1960). Review. *The New Statesman*, June.

Brubacher, J. S. (1977). *On the Philosophy of Higher Education*. San Francisco, Jossey-Bass.

Carr, G. R. (1974). Karl Jaspers as an intellectual critic. D.Phil. thesis, University of Birmingham.

Hamilton, M. L. (1976). Jaspers and Freud – Coleridge Revividus. *Manchester Literary and Philosophical Society, Memoirs and Proceedings* **117**, 26–36.

Jaspers, K. (1923). *Der Idee der Universität*. Berlin, Springer-Verlag.

Jaspers, K. (1951). *Man in the Modern Age*. London, Routledge and Kegan Paul.

Jaspers, K. (1953). *The Origin and Goal of History*. London, Routledge and Kegan Paul.

Jaspers, K. (1959). *Truth and Symbol*. New York, Twayne.

Jaspers, K. (1960). *The Idea of the University*. London, Peter Owen.

Jaspers, K. (1963). *Philosophy and the World*. Chicago, Regnery.

Jaspers, K. (1969). *Philosophy*, Vol. 1. Chicago, University of Chicago Press.

Niblett, W. R. (1964). On existentialism and education. *British Journal of Educational Studies*, **2** (2), 101.

Olsen, A. M. (1979). *Transcendence and Hermeneutics: An Interpretation of the Philosophy of Karl Jaspers*. The Hague, Martinus Nijhoff.

Schilpp, P. A. (Ed.) (1957). *The Philosophy of Karl Jaspers*. New York, Tudor.

Wallraff, C. F. (1970). *Karl Jaspers: An Introduction to His Philosophy*. Princeton, Princeton University Press.

Wilcher, L. (1960). Review. *Universities Quarterly*, **15** (1), 79ff.

5

Max Horkheimer: A Justification for a Social Research Institute – 'To Serve the Truth Relentlessly'

The authors that have already been considered have produced enough examples of the dilemmas facing the mid-twentieth-century university for an indication or a set of tendencies or trends to emerge. These tendencies became firm directions by the second half of the century. Thus, in our times, we are familiar with critical judgements on liberal views, and their failure. We are also proud to be hard-nosed about optimism. The current attitude is to be sceptical of the belief that more education will mean less human suffering or that education can be an adequate consolation for the flowing tide of misery. On an epistemological level, it is almost a cliché to castigate the lack of reality in standard categorizations of subject boundaries. We are sophisticated in our knowledge of the power that supports and maintains subject departmentalism, to the detriment of wholeness and 'reality'. The corporate university, as the agent of a powerful state apparatus, next looms in the catalogue of sins of higher education. Finally, there is distrust and suspicion of the ambiguity of the role of the intellectual. Is he or she a free-wheeler, committed participant or a critical observer? Who can tell whether the intellectual is duped or duper? All these, by now familiar aspects of the criticism of the late twentieth-century university, were raised and, in an individual manner, had solutions offered by the writer who is to occupy attention in this chapter, Max Horkheimer. Both his writing and his experience as an academic leader led to a proposal to bridge apparent opposites and to span dualisms.

The key text: The Inaugural Lecture by the Director of the Frankfurt Institute

Max Horkheimer provides us with a key text of considerable value, since he writes about the construction of a new higher education institution almost from its inception. The text is the inaugural lecture delivered to mark Horkheimer's installation as the Director of the Frankfurt Institute for Social Research in 1931. Carl Grunberg, his predecessor, had been virtually the first director of the

School, an independent research centre for social research, from 1924 to 1929, the actual director having died soon after taking office in 1922. Horkheimer was appointed at a crucial juncture in German intellectual and political history, and it is largely owing to his vision and perseverance in fulfilling that vision that the school was able to survive closure by the Nazis in 1933, its subsequent exile in Switzerland and the USA, and its return to Germany in 1950. The achievements of the Frankfurt School, as it came to be called, are well known and thoroughly documented in English (see Jay 1973; Held 1980; Kolakowski 1978), but the key text examined here (Horkheimer 1931) provides a theoretical justification for the success that followed. It is rare to be able to work on a blueprint so consistent with the edifice which was erected on it. Horkheimer's style and his painstaking analysis encourage the metaphors of planning and construction, because of the apparent logic and orderliness of his argument. The summary that follows illustrates most of the themes that I pursue in the rest of this chapter using other texts in addition.

The central argument of the address is about the organization of the curriculum around a central unifying discipline which translates as 'social philosophy' (*Sozialphilosophie*). Horkheimer defines this area of study, for which there is no simple parallel in English intellectual history, as the philosophical explanation of man's fate, not merely the fate of man as an individual but of man as a member of a community. In an orderly manner, the speaker traces the history of social philosophy with its individualistic roots in Kant and, more powerfully for man as a social being, in Hegel. The neglect of this discipline after Hegel arose from a false atmosphere of optimism and individualism supporting material progress. Eventually, the 'scorned metaphysics wreaks a terrible revenge' when the age's confidence faltered. Social philosophy was then revived but only as a 'retreat from the present state of knowledge' and a false source of consolation. We shall return later to this important point that the unifying subject of the curriculum is not a therapy but a stimulus for a new way of seeing.

Having led his audience to the present times, Horkheimer defined the core of his curricular theory. It is that social philosophy would be concerned with the concrete world of research. In this central proposition he is also, of course, making a statement about the nature and function of an institution of higher education. Social philosophy should not be confused with the disciplines which actually examine and record the concrete world. It is not to be assumed to be the same as sociology or one of the other social sciences. What social philosophy can do, however, is to say things about the worth of a social science discipline's activity. It will inevitably attend to the universal and the essential, and in so doing 'give life' to particular research. The essential bias of this curricular proposal lies in this relationship between the unifying discipline and 'other' disciplines. Horkheimer asks his audience to avoid the polarization of the theoretical and practical. Instead, he proposes 'a continuing dialectical interpenetration of philosophical theory and the praxis of particular disciplines' (Horkheimer 1931).

At this point of the address the argument ceases to be concerned with the way subjects or disciplines might infuse each other. The epistemological discussion changes and is concerned with the nature of the institution. Horkheimer sees the ideal institution as an essential setting for 'lasting communal relationships' between those disciplines concerned with social problems, such as economics, sociology, history and psychology. The team of social scientists will engage in a continuous dialectical process. The task of the leader of the Institute is to make this collaboration effective and continuous. The director's power to act effectively in this way is to be exercised in maintaining his independent role in the way already established by his predecessors. The address concludes with an example of how the Institute will operate under his rule. Traditionally, the age-old questions of the interrelationships between the economic life of society, the psychology of the individual and the cultural life of the community have failed to be explored with success. The reason for this failure is that separate disciplines have studied the problem with an 'uncritical and superannuated division of spirit and reality', a division which is 'naively postulated as absolute', and thus the researchers are 'spared the trouble of particular scientific problems. They avoid consciously or unconsciously, the complexities of relating spirit and reality dialectically.' The Institute would tackle the question in a different manner by concentrating on specific research sectors (such as on the skilled workers in Germany) and will ask questions about the economics, the psychology of the individual and the culture of that specific setting. The 'world-view' will not be lost. It will help those who are engaged in the detailed and particular to ask the right questions.

In many ways, Horkheimer might easily be eligible for the considerable criticisms listed in the first paragraph of this chapter. The very institution that he is to head is a research institution. It is pardonable to conclude that it is partial by definition, being concerned with subject areas which are merely elements of a more complex educational picture. As a privately funded institution, it relied on the profits of industry and commerce and was a miniature precursor of corporate institutions of the future and, furthermore, set out with what might be said to be a Utopian vision of a future based on social science. In practice, the new Director opposes all these trends and recognizes the rocks underneath the boat he is guiding through the dangerous shallows. I referred earlier to Horkheimer as someone who brought together opposites, and indeed a reading of his work leaves one with more positive feelings than with negative criticisms. I shall concentrate on four linked features of his vision, all of which lead, as with other thinking in this book, to a doctrine of hope.

The nature of human knowledge: Wholeness and unity

The theme of 'wholeness' in the sphere of knowledge is as old as German philosophy itself, but the distinctive mark of the Frankfurt School is paradoxically the recognition of individual subject areas in the social sciences at the same time as the essential requirement of interdisciplinarity. Jay (1973: 298) says 'It was the only interdisciplinary aggregation of scholars working on different

problems from a common theoretical base, to coalesce in modern times.'
Horkheimer sought to provide in the study called 'social philosophy' a curricular key to interdependence. Furthermore, this linking subject was not only at the
level of a theoretical underpinning for further theoretical justification, but a
genuinely worked out range of studies for a working, productive Institute of
social science. Jay (1973) and Held (1980) illustrate in detail how the history of
the school demonstrated the energy put into attempts to link differing social
science studies and differing methodologies and the success that was achieved.

More significant for our purpose than the history of the Institute as an
interdisciplinary setting, is the procedure put forward by Horkheimer. The
important point was that the collaborating disciplines come together in a spirit
of openness. The activity, as we have seen in the summary above, was
communal. In *Zum Problem der Wahrheit*, Horkheimer distinguishes between two
phases of social enquiry, *Darstellungsweise* and *Forschung*. The first-named can be
translated as 'presentation' or 'representation'; its purpose is to locate the part
in the context of a totality. The second phrase is equivalent to the term 'research'
in English. Research is a consequence of the placing of the part within the whole
rather than a segment cut from the whole body of knowledge and experience.

One major criticism that might be levelled at this scheme of interdisciplinarity is that the unifying subject, social philosophy, acts as a censorious, rigid
controller dominating and perverting the true functions of the collaborating
disciplines. It is important therefore to grasp with Horkheimer that social
philosophy is an open and flexible discipline in itself. In sections of the address,
and even more significantly in the major work *Zum Problem der Wahrheit*,
Horkheimer is keen to reassure his audience that each thought (or to use his own
phrases 'particular knowledge', 'expression of truth') will not have an *a priori*
meaning and value, but will 'in a particular historical moment form factors of a
force that changes the world' (Arato and Gebhardt 1978: 236). In the inaugural
address, Horkheimer emphasizes that for him, and hence for social philosophy,
there are no generally valid truths, but there are 'positions or stances'. In a later
work he was to compare his theory with Hegel's. Whereas Hegel is said to have
suffered from a concluded (*abgeschlossen*) view of history, his own proposed
process of scholarship was an unconcluded dialectic (*unabgeschlossene Dialektik*):
'An isolated and conclusive reality is unthinkable.' This reservation about the
permanence of truth (conditional certainty) would awaken echoes of the
uncertainty principle in the physical sciences, as Horkheimer was well aware.

If isolation and conclusiveness were unthinkable in intellectual, epistemological terms, even more unacceptable was the division within man himself
caused by divisive thinking. In 'On the problem of truth', Horkheimer castigates the intellectual's lop-sided critical development, so that scholars 'develop
high level critical faculties in a special branch of science, while remaining on the
level of a backward group in respect of the question of social life and echoing the
most ignorant phrases' (Arato and Gebhardt 1978: 411). Horkheimer claims
that this strange asymmetrical form of human being is a product of bourgeois
social order. Whole belief is one thing, science and mathematical 'accuracy' are
another, so that there is a deadly 'dual relationship to truth'. The modern

scholar is at one and the same time capable of admitting the relative and conditional nature of truth but meanwhile firmly espousing specialist scholarly truth. What then can unite? Is it the special cement of a distinct subject – a new form of philosophy dignified with the title of *Sozial Philosophie* – which can act as the only uniting factor?

The Institute and interdisciplinarity

I believe that in the practical working out of the theory of the Frankfurt School, in the very act of attempting to create a whole view and in attempting to make fully rounded truth come to light, an atmosphere of unity was engendered:

> There is no eternal riddle of the world, no world secret, the penetration of which once and for all would be the mission of thought . . . Rather the truth is advanced because human beings who possess it stand by it unbendingly, apply it and carry it through, act accordingly to it and bring it to power against the resistance of reactionary, narrow, one-sided points of view. (Arato and Gebhardt 1978: 421–2)

The unity is achieved by the consistent stance taken by the company of scholars, educated in this tradition. Furthermore, this quotation gives a very important indication of the educated human being that Horkheimer proposes – a person of action, of will and of courage, as against a passive receptor educated by a curriculum of devices and mechanisms, of inputs and outputs. It says something too about the nature of the institution which serves those individuals, a topic to which we must eventually return. For the moment, let us instead turn to the process of interdisciplinarity and the attitude that the ideal scholar will employ to bring together into a rounded whole the many one-sided facets left isolated in the modern dispersion of ideas.

There has been considerable attention paid to the Frankfurt School in its post-1940 manifestations, and particularly with the names of Horkheimer and Adorno (reinforced by the 'modernisations' of their work in the late 1960s and early 1970s revival of Marxist theory). It is therefore easy to neglect what we are looking at here in its early simpler beginning. Indeed, concentration on the changes that occur in such well debated concepts as *Kritische Theorie* from 1931 through the disillusionment of 1936 and onward to the full limelight of 35 years or so later, can blind us to some of the simpler things that were being said at the inauguration of the school, which is, after all, our *point d'appui*. The theories underpinning the scholarly attitude and the function of the institution of education was one of harmony. Harmony was alive and well at this early stage of the Frankfurt School's formation, as much as in later fully developed stages. What distinguishes the statements of 1931 from those of 1936 and later is the high tide of hope soon to ebb in disillusionment as totalitarian systems grew in strength and, even more significantly, in public support. It is this very issue of public opinion which engages the new director as he sets out the early programme for the school. Social philosophy, the kernel of the curriculum, the unifying element that forms the main theme of the discourse in 1931, is in fact both a formative and a receptive agent of public opinion. As Jay points out, social philosophy is not a single *Wissenschaft* in search of immutable truth, but it is 'understood as a materialist theory enriched and supplemented by empirical work' (Jay 1973: 25). Social philosophy is thus a highly charged synthesizing agent, with its energy coming from a critical attitude to public affairs. Connerton (1980), in a thorough study of the Frankfurt School, gives the enquiring reader an important interpretation of its place in the German tradition derived from the Enlightenment. He suggests that for Horkheimer and Adorno, public opinion can be interpreted in two ways. One is as a potentially critical agency and the other as a receptive organ, easily engineered and manipulated. The function of social philosophy was to encourage and renew the first and to apply its criticism to the second.

What we see, therefore, is a two-way process between social public life and the scholar in the institution. It is, however, not a mere transference of information from the life of action to the contemplative receiver. The process is a dialectic one, both between scholars in the Institute and between the Institute and the active world. As we noted at the beginning of this chapter, Horkheimer's significance in the history of higher education is that he bridged hitherto irreconcilable polarities. So science as theory and science as practice were not to be opposed but brought into active dialogue through the Institute. Particular disciplines, such as sociology, political theory and economics were necessary to explore social practice from their distinct positions with their distinctive techniques, but the end of the story, or rather its beginning, was the bringing together of these partial truths strengthened in bonding by the force of the institution and by the device of a core area of thought. Thus the Institute's task in its meeting with society is to set out the truth but, again, not to proclaim with partial commitment. As we shall see in the next paragraphs, the Institute's stance and that of its members must be to deliver to the public world in a critical manner the reality as it appears, but not to commit themselves to a final version.

The ideal organization

The institutional structure (if that is not too firm a word for the Institute's actual rather loose and changing historical form) is closely related by intention and by history to the stance identified in the last paragraph. In the inaugural address we see the new director emphasizing two things. First, he wishes to continue his predecessor's doctrine of 'the dictatorship of the Director'. This half-humorous phrase conveys the central position of the person whose principal duty is to make the disciplines relate to each other, to a central set of values and to perceived social problems. The director was, in short, not to be an 'organization man'. As his subsequent publications illustrate, he was frequently personally engaged in the Institute's collaborative ventures either by joint authorship or, in the Institute's journal (*Zeitschrift für Sozialforschung*) in published discussion with other scholars.

The second emphasis in the address is on the independent position of the Institute. At this stage in its history it was not part of the University of Frankfurt. Financially independent, because of the support of the Weil family, the Institute was enabled to remain detached from the encumbered and compromised attitudes of universities which owed their existence to the state's patronage. Edward Shils points out in an article, which, *inter alia*, is about Horkheimer's continuous leadership in intellectual circles, that institutions 'create a resonant and echoing intellectual environment' (Shils 1979: 762). In the case of the Institute, the unison sung by its intellectual environment was to harmonize its member scholars into a community of specialists who were not merely gathered together by geographical accident in one place, but committed to a dialogue with each other. More pointedly, this grouping of intellectuals might be called a deliberately marginal community. The Institute, despite its origins in the many currents of thought emanating from Marxism, avoided any political affiliation (although individual members of the Institute did join political parties). Kolakowski dubs it 'an important para-Marxist movement' (Kolakowski 1978: 341). The phrase often associated with scholars in the Institute, *nicht mitzumachen* (not to join in) was, therefore, not a withdrawal from a public role for social sciences, but a deliberate stance of separateness in order to be more usefully available to tackle the world's problems. Inevitably this position has brought upon members of the Institute the criticism of being negative, anti-progressive and anti-technological. This early address shows that, on the contrary, Horkheimer is giving his colleagues a vision of the quality that modern life could at its best sustain. When, in 1954, Horkheimer returned to Frankfurt, he was to emphasize that technological progress was not in itself the enemy which threatens the spirit, and today, even the material survival of humanity. What is the enemy, is the wrong choice of priorities resulting in technology not being made subservient to human goals. This part of the discussion leads directly to a few thoughts on the legitimization of an institution of higher education in a modern society.

Higher education and society: What is the Institute for?

In our contemporary intellectual scene, the arguments of justification tend to be either on economic or on cultural grounds. Horkheimer's justification for the institution he was to lead was weighted towards the political and the deeply moral. Early in the address we have seen him reject the role of philosophy as a form of consolation for the ills of modern life. As we have seen, he explored the unhappy history of social philosophy as a device for what he terms 'transfiguring' the harsh realities of modern society. It is his firm view that reassurance, consolation and therapy were inadequate justifications for the intellectual's task. In the famous *Dialectic of the Enlightenment*, at the end of the chapter entitled 'Juliette, or enlightenment and morality', Adorno and Horkheimer remind us of

Nietzsche's answer to the question, 'Where do your greatest dangers lie?' – 'In compassion'.

> With this denial he redeemed the unshakeable confidence in man that is constantly betrayed by every form of assurance that seeks only to console. (Adorno and Horkheimer 1979: 119)

If consolation is not the aim of an intellectual institution, what should it be? The aim of this gathering of intellectuals is to provide 'an overview', but not solely in order to be above the world. The scholar engaged in the dialectical process is compelled forward in two ways. First, his engagement is likely to change what he sees. Such an outcome is inevitably political, so the first function of the institution is to challenge the existing political order. Second, he is impelled by a moral force to inform the world of this new vision. The institution of higher education has therefore the potential to be a radical agent for change. Indeed, when the sore state of the modern world is objectively surveyed, the need for such an institution, given a moral basis of regard for humanity and its potential, becomes more evident.

Conclusion: The relevance of the 1930s experiment

In conclusion, let us concentrate on the relevance of this early work of Horkheimer to the many issues facing those engaged in higher education today. So much has changed since that January day of the inaugural in 1931. In any case, the Institute was a 'peculiar organization', a small group of scholars, independently financed and organized in a highly individual, even idiosyncratic way. For a significant period of time it functioned in exile in a host country at war. Furthermore, the Institute was particular in its limited range of work, a specialized social science 'cell'. It cannot be compared with other wider ranging institutions, such as universities with many and varied disciplines and more complex organizational structures. Despite these disclaimers, a number of points do claim contemporary attention.

The importance of thinking through and setting out for debate the theoretical underpinning of curricular interdisciplinarity must be encouraged in all institutions that aspire to link subjects or to provide a web of knowledge. The proposition in Horkheimer's address of a central unifying discipline is not new. One has only to consider, in writings in English, Ortega's proposal for cultural studies as a 'core discipline' or, in more partisan spirit, F. R. Leavis's proposal for English literature as a central subject of the curriculum (see Chapter 6). An equally rich area of study is the creation of new universities in the UK in the 1960s, some of which aimed to create a new 'map of knowledge'. It is also interesting to note in British specialist 'monotechnic' institutions, such as theological colleges or teacher-training colleges from the 1950s to 1970, a continuing debate on the best means of preparing graduate professionals who are required by external professional authorities to study a wide range of subjects in their training. In the case of the colleges for training priests, the role of theology as a 'unifier' deserves attention (see, for example, Baelz 1975). The value of Horkheimer's argument is less in proposing any particular subject as a catalyst or as a unifier, but more in proposing that the collaborating disciplines should engage jointly both within the institution and outside it, by asking questions concerned with value and by engaging with the relationship between the subject methodology and the society in which the university or research institution is placed. Finally, one group within the institution may have to be responsible for making all this happen, and this in turn raises questions of academic control and the relative power of subject disciplines in their inter-relationships.

Equally important for modern consideration is the importance of an institutional structure which demands (not merely 'encourages') a dialogue between disciplines. The history of the Institute itself is a reassurance to those who look for a collaboration between disciplines, because in the years it operated we are told that the disciplines did not have their individuality destroyed. So often extinction of hard-won individuality is felt to be the threat under many interdisciplinary proposals. On the contrary, in this scheme, the individual discipline is valued for its intrinsic worth. It is the engagement in two directions, with 'social fact' and with other disciplines in a dialectic exchange that marks Horkheimer's proposal as being of permanent value to educationalists.

Finally, I have found in Horkheimer's thesis, as in other writers in this selection, a most important permanent essence, not in great supply in universities and colleges at this moment. Again, this is the quality of hope. Education is not, however, intended to produce false hope, nor to provide escape, comfort and solace. Some modern popular political writings about education in general assume that learning is a form of therapy or a way of absorbing the energies of a leisured generation. Nothing could be further from the aims of this Institute. Horkheimer sets the Institute an active, critical goal which is far from remote and ivory-towered. He was to express this very clearly in a later work:

> Rather the truth is advanced because the human beings who possess it stand by it unbendingly, apply it and carry it through, act according to it, and bring it to power against the resistance of reactionary, narrow one-sided points of view (Arato and Gebhardt 1978: 422).

A study of the responses of universities, polytechnics and colleges to recent financial constraints in Britain does not reveal an unvarying regard for their purpose as an 'unbending' power against 'reactionary, narrow one-sided points of view'. Perhaps we are wrong to look for it in our own anguished times of contraction, when more pragmatic solutions are likely to carry the argument. At least we may remind ourselves that 1931, when Max Horkheimer delivered his lecture, was an equally inauspicious time for German intellectuals. So much attention has been paid to the Frankfurt School's reputation in the 1960s and early 1970s, when it was patently destructively critical of modern culture and of modern society, that it is easy to forget the positive creative aspects of its programme which its director was to set out so clearly in his inaugural. His final words would serve as a useful motto for any institution of higher education. He reminded his audience of the 'impulse to a world-view' spoken of by his predecessor, Grunberg. Horkheimer suggested, on his own account, where that world view would lead his new Institute: 'to the unshakeable will to serve the truth relentlessly' (Horkheimer 1931). The fact that the Frankfurt School was in the future to spend much effort in persuading everyone that 'truth' is a slippery concept to pursue, and that it is always problematic, does not reduce the power of this inaugural clarion call. The word 'serve' is important. For Horkheimer, as for Jaspers, the role of the institution was to be of service to truth, passionately and relentlessly, a service of clarification.

References

Arato, A. and Gebhardt, E. (Eds) (1978). *The Essential Frankfurt School Reader*. New York, Citizen Books.

Adorno, T. and Horkheimer, M. (1979). *Dialectic of the Enlightenment*. London, Verso.

Baelz, P. (1975). *Theology as an Integrating Discipline*. London, Church Office of Information.

Connerton, P. (1980). *The Tragedy of Enlightenment: An Essay on the Frankfurt School*. Cambridge, Cambridge University Press.

Held, D. (1980). *Introduction to Critical Theory*. London, Hutchinson.

Horkheimer, M. (1931). Die Gegenwartige Lage der Sozialphilosophie und die Aufgeben eines Institute. In *Frankfurter Universitatsreden*, **xxxvii**.

Jay, M. (1973). *The Dialectical Imagination: A History of the Frankfurt School and the Institute of Social Research, 1923–1950*. London, Heinemann.

Kolakowski, L. (1978). *Main Currents of Marxism*, Vol. 3 (translated). Oxford, Clarendon Press.

Shils, E. (1979). Tradition, ecology and institution in the history of sociology. *Daedalus*, **99**.

6

F. R. Leavis: The University as a 'Creative Centre of Civilization' – The Idea of an English School

This chapter is unlike the others because it is not about the educational writing of a professional philosopher. The writer considered here was a literary critic with no pretensions in that direction; indeed, he held strongly antagonistic views on some professional philosophers of his time. Frank Richard Leavis was a teacher of English literature in the University of Cambridge from 1927. He never held a chair in that University, only becoming Reader at the age of 65. His influence among those studying English at the University was, however, considerable, but even more powerfully his writing in major critical works (such as *New Bearings in English Poetry, The Common Pursuit, The Great Tradition* and on major studies of Charles Dickens and D. H. Lawrence) was profound. Generations of students of literature all over the world were and are influenced by his perceptions. He and his wife, Q. D. Leavis, with a circle of fellow critics, initially exercised their influence through a journal called *Scrutiny* published between 1934 and 1953. Many of the contributions to *Scrutiny* were expanded into publications in their own right. The 'key text' which we shall consider in this chapter grew from this very source.

The key text: *Education and the University: A Sketch for an 'English School'*

This text, published in 1943, is like the work of Ortega and of Jaspers, a product of a time of war, but having its origins in the crisis that led to the conflict. The original source for the book was an article in *Scrutiny* (September 1934) entitled 'Why universities?' Articles of a similar nature appeared in the same period. Leavis himself reviewed an educational experiment by Dr Meiklejohn of the University of Wisconsin in the first edition of *Scrutiny*, which was to be re-used in the work of 1943. Other writers raised related topics, such as E. W. F. Tomlin on Oxford's 'Modern greats', H. A. Mason on revision of the study of the classics and L. C. Knights on 'Mr C. S. Lewis and the status quo'. Later, in 1939, Q. D. Leavis wrote on 'The function of the university'. These pieces were all in tune

with the book *Education and the University*. There was indeed a common tone
about the articles and the book, established as early as the first edition of *Scrutiny*.
As Leavis himself remembered years later, its purpose was 'to make a difference
in history' (Leavis 1963: 1). The first volume announced more specifically that a
'revolution in education' was planned.

More directly perhaps than any other writer in this collection, Leavis was to
continue the campaign to reorganize the idea of a university over a long period
after the publication of the major text. The thesis was restated and modernized
in 1967 in the Clark Lectures. I shall comment below on the additional material
provided by the adaptation of these later lectures into a book (Leavis 1967). In a
sense, Leavis and his wife always returned in all their work to the central issues
of the place of an English school and the importance of the university in national
life. Public events appear not to have altered or even moderated the views which
they held in the 1930s. On the contrary, the reader finds that they confirmed
their position as the century progresses. The Leavises would have regarded
'progresses' as an inadequate term. As far as they were concerned, the passing
years were a descent into a seriously deteriorated state. So, at the end of the
1960s, in lectures in the USA, there is a continued consistent statement about
the university 'as a focus of consciousness and human responsibility' (Leavis
and Leavis 1969). Also in that decade, occurred the well-publicized, open
disagreement with Lord Snow about 'Two Cultures'. Leavis' scorn for the
proposition, propounded by Lord Snow, that science and the arts were dangerously divided and that education should be reformed to reunite them, gave the
literacy critic a further opportunity to restate his case for what he regarded as
the central humanitarian discipline of the study of literature. It is to that
argument that I shall now turn.

As I have said above, *Education and the University* began with a review of an
'experimental college'. Leavis found much to admire in the American experiment, although he believed it had fundamental flaws. Rapidly leaving behind
the actual source that inspired this essay, he expresses a fundamental belief in
universities as 'recognised symbols of cultural tradition'. Indeed, as he repeated
in other contexts, 'if something effective cannot be done at that level, it would
seem vain to hope much of efforts in education at other levels' (Leavis 1943: 16).
At other times, Leavis uses the words 'foci' or 'centre' for the universities as a
force capable of 'exercising enormous influence'. The authority they exercise
'could check and control the blind drive onward of material and mechanical
development with its human consequences'. The virtue of the universities in this
defensive role against modern forces is that they have the strength of their
history and continuity. Their origins are within 'concrete and historical
England'. If the universities represent reality grounded in a tradition, literature
and its critical study represent an even more grounded sphere of activity, based
as they are on the 'most intimate kind of study' of that tradition.

The opposition to these two liberal powers, the university and the study of
literature, arises from the very forces that generate the ills of modern society. It
is no use, Leavis argues, imposing a scheme, such as T. S. Eliot's vision of a
Christian community onto the complex, interrelated sicknesses of this century.

Nor is it useful to imagine a return to simpler, older social structures, such as rural, medieval culture. Leavis's list of society's ills would not be strange to a reader of Ortega y Gasset. The enormous technical complexity of the modern world requires a correspondingly gigantic co-ordination by an administrative system. This dreadful modern combination he called the 'technologico-Benthamite world' in later works. The leaders of labour and the nation's statesmen are alike, inadequate to handle this massive task. Simple, short-term solutions are established by them to ensure that the machinery is, at least, smooth running. Only the university can effectively handle the task which is:

> to explore the means of bringing the various essential kinds of specialist knowledge and training into effective relation with informed general intelligence, humane culture, social conscience and political will. (Leavis 1943: 24)

The universities, however, share similar symptoms with the sick society in which they are placed. Their two chief solutions to the world's problems in reality create more difficulties. They feel, on the one hand, that they are required to produce narrow specialists to solve the inadequate operation of a technocratic society, but they are not clear what kind of people can emerge from such systems. The opposite solution, appealing to some, is to educate 'broadly' in order to produce Renaissance Man in the twentieth century; an impossible task doomed from the start.

Having established the diagnosis, Leavis proposes a cure. In the preface to the second edition of the text of 1943, he is at pains to emphasize that the reform of English teaching is inseparable from the reform of the university. Both must be reconstructed so that a renewed vigour can be felt in the nation as a whole. His proposals, by the time of the second edition, are put forward to influence a wider sphere than English literature at Oxford or Cambridge. In 1943, however, he started from the presumption that the oldest universities have important advantages as a base for reform. The ancient seats of learning represent the essential virtue of continuity ('carrying on and fostering the essential life of a time-honoured and powerful institution'). Like Cardinal Newman, Leavis believed that Oxford and Cambridge were uniquely favoured in creating the context for informal, but powerful education:

> . . . the stimulus derived from the general ambience, to the education got in that school of unspecialised intelligence, which is created in informal intercourse – intercourse that brings together intellectual appetites from specialists of all kinds, and from various academic levels. (Leavis 1943: 28)

They are 'so much more' than educational institutions, aiming not to produce specialists or generally educated men, but 'specialists who are in touch with a humane centre'. Leavis refers to Ortega y Gasset at this point to share his judgement on the stupidity of the specialist. All is not, however, to be left to the chance combination of ancient 'ethos' and the good fortune of the students rubbing shoulders with people of different backgrounds. The university must make some definite and deliberate provision in order to bring specialism into contact with 'a real centre'. This centre is the humane heart of the university and it is occupied in Leavis' scheme by the English school.

The reader who comes to Leavis' work without the benefit of reading and thinking with others about his literary criticism will find his statement about the discipline of literary criticism strangely argued. They are obviously tinged with strong feelings, even with whiffs of gunpowder from previous literary engagements. Too frequently, Leavis appeals to some elusive shared sense, which is plainly more than 'common' sense, being distinguished in its quality of experience. A favourite rhetorical device is to say that a critical point is hardly worth making, or to assert that anyone with a small amount of attention to literature will identify a flaw in an argument. Despite this irritating style, Leavis does set out more plainly in these educational texts, perhaps more than in his genuinely critical work, the qualities of the 'discipline' of literary criticism, which is to be the effective centre for humanizing the modern university.

In the first place, the discipline of this vital subject is integral to itself. It is not imported from linguistics or philology. Those are 'Ersatz methods', giving a false air of scholarship to English studies. The true discipline trains 'intelligence' and sensibility at the same time. The ideal student becomes critically sensitive but capable of making a precise response. This is not a simple analytical ability, for it integrates diverse elements. Finally, the student requires powers of pertinacity. He or she must have staying power as well as delicacy. There can be no fixed or predetermined outcomes, so courage is required as well as a sense of self-direction. In short, the good student has a 'prospecting and ranging mind'. These capacities must remind any reader of Newman's aims for the education of character. In another context, these are the qualities which a politician might claim as valuable for future leaders of society. Leavis is fully aware that he is specifying the values required for the future leadership and improvement of society as a whole. The actual processes of reform of the university's structure need not detain us here, except to note that, as with Ortega and Jaspers, there is a sketch of a curriculum (in this case based ingeniously on a wide-ranging study of the seventeenth century). Leavis is keen to propose a reform of the assessment system of his own university, proposing new schemes of course work assessment based on critical reading. In fact, the acquisition of the skill of reading is at the heart of the discipline of an English school. A long appendix to the text is a reworking of a response he had made previously to Ezra Pound's pamphlet, *How to Read*.

So, in summary, we see here a proposal for undergraduate studies. Like Horkheimer, who proposed a scheme with a fundamental discipline of *Sozialphilosophie*, Leavis demands that a specific subject area should act as a centre studies. Unlike Horkheimer, he is not proposing a programme of postgraduate research and developments, nor is he as clear as the director of the Frankfurt Institute about the way in which the specialisms would take their place in a hierarchy of study relating to the central core subject. Plainly, Leavis proposes that all specialists will have the benefit of literary studies, which in its turn will colour their own specialisms. The specialisms do not disappear, nor are they merged into some generalized 'cultural mixture'. The Cambridge tripos (the formal system of assessment, usually at the end of the second year of a three-year first degree and at the end of the course) could in his view be adapted to include literary studies as well as specialist studies. English studies include a range of material far wider than traditional literary genres, and therefore, as we would say today, 'access' is possible for all who are intelligent and perceptive enough to wish to learn. In a lecture many years later, Leavis was to say:

> Some day, perhaps, I shall permit myself to brag of the psychologist, the mediaevalist, the anthropologist, the critic of French literature, and so on, distinguished in their respective lines, who once 'read English' with me. (Singh 1986: 181)

The development of the idea of an English 'centre'

The later work, *English Literature in our Time and the University* (Leavis 1967), elaborates the ideas of the war-time publication. Elaboration was required for a number of reasons. First, his earlier.work had received the criticism that, throughout his life, he seemed both to enjoy and bewail. Misunderstandings had to be cleared away. Therefore, he defends himself, and *en passant* Matthew Arnold, against the charge that 'civilizing', cultural activities did not save the Third Reich from creating Belsen and Dachau. He typically responds by labelling the criticisms as 'unintelligence'. He had never asserted that 'culture' would be so generally spread that perfect societies would result. He proposed in the 1960s, as in the 1930s, a spiritual continuity with the best in civilizing and humanitarian traditions extended tactically into the inimical environment of modern times. Similarly, he rejects the criticism of the reviewer who believed he was proposing that courses in literary criticism will create artists and, in particular, writers. Of course, agreed Leavis, most of the famous creative artists never went to university. However, the cultural atmosphere in which they operated as artists had been profoundly influenced by the universities of their own time and of their predecessors. One important channel of influence was the development of the language, which, in their turn, the writers of genius used and influenced. They did not, however, create that language.

A second major change in the 30 years elapsing between the two books was the growth and diversification of university studies. Not only does Leavis continue to criticize Lord Snow, in the later work he reserves some arrows for Lord Robbins, whose report of 1963 prepared the way for a major expansion of higher education in the UK. Leavis was scornful of suggestions for 'mixed courses' or for palliative attempts to teach scientists some English literature or to teach students of humanities in science laboratories. Indeed, the apparently commonsense divisions of people into specialist subject disciplines, exemplified particularly by the 'Two Cultures' thesis, is another example of 'technico-Benthamite' simplification at work. The need for a subject area, English literature, which preserves a 'full continuity of mind, spirit and sensibility' became, in his view, more, not less, vital at a time of rapid expansion of student numbers and proliferation of institutions and of courses within them.

A third area of change between the two texts on the ideal university arises from one powerfully developing influence. On reading the texts side by side, one is struck by the important role played by T. S. Eliot in the second, later work. Leavis had engaged over the years after the war with someone whom he regarded as a major thinker (which equates in his vocabularly with 'critic'), as well as poet and dramatist. Chapters three and four of the Clark Lectures are mainly taken up with studies of Eliot. Chapter five is concerned with another significant figure in Leavis' list of great creative artists, D. H. Lawrence. Significantly, it is not Lawrence the novelist, but Lawrence as the critic of *Hamlet*, that occupies this chapter. What Leavis is saying of both Eliot and Lawrence is of importance for our understanding of the part English would play in his ideal university. To separate 'critic' from 'poet' or 'novelist' in these cases is to polarize creative capabilities and to feed the very rigid methods of teaching English which Leavis wishes to reform. The study of Eliot raises two issues which are implicit but underdeveloped in the war-time text, but very explicit 24 years later: the sense of a community of learning and the vital nature of a common inheritance of language.

A good teacher, to Leavis, is 'One who has the kinds of interest in literature that go with finding pleasure and profit in discussing it with intelligent young students' (Leavis 1967: 66). This statement is more than a general expression of good practice in tutorial work. (We shall leave for the moment the implications of 'intelligent young students'.) The implicity collaborative activity of teaching arises from the implicity collaborative activity of reading a poem. The word 'collaborative' is frequently used in this text. The poem should be available for all, but a process of renewing a living whole occurs when it is read 'collaboratively'. Those who participate in the process will 'perpetuate what they participate in'. This ideal process of learning in a three-fold partnership – teacher, student and poem – leads to what Leavis now calls a 'third realm'. The creation of this realm is increasingly urgent in 1967. It is a territory which technologico-Benthamites either ignore or despise, but:

> Our business, our vital need, is to maintain the continuity of life and consciousness that a cultural tradition is, and not to lose anything essential from our heritage – the heritage that is only kept alive by creative renewal (which means change) in every present. (Leavis 1967: 184)

Eliot's Essays (Eliot 1932) were first published as a collection in 1932, with major additions in 1934 and 1951. The history of that seminal selection of criticism is contemporary with the successive editions of *Scrutiny* and also with Leavis' early major criticism. There is a more significant parallel in the content of the essays. Like Leavis, Eliot ranged widely in his critical vision. The opening essay (reprinted from 1919) is 'Tradition and individual talent'. The collection ends in an essay of 1932 entitled 'Modern education and the classics', covering in between not only literary criticism of Elizabethan and Jacobean drama but also a wide range of writers and, again like Leavis, topics on the quality of modern life. The interest in theology is, of course, Eliot's preserve, not Leavis', but in that context, Eliot is exploring tradition. It is the Church as a community that he explores, rather than the nature of religious experience. *The Idea of a Christian Society* (Eliot 1939) is further evidence of Eliot's concern for the interrelationship of a culture's beliefs and the institutions that sustain them. Like Leavis, he concentrated on language as the living, changing demonstration of hidden (and vulnerable) springs within English life.

If Eliot is to share the responsibility for some of the influences which encouraged the development of Leavis' ideas of the value of an ideal academic community, Matthew Arnold must have some credit for reinforcing Leavis' consistently held view of the 'living tradition' of literature in England. He also owes to Arnold the grim vision of the Philistine attack on the true culture. This depressing prospect is expressed even more forcibly in 1967 than in 1943. Arnold, he reminds us, could rely on an educated public who attended to prophecies like *Culture and Anarchy*. This public has now decayed; therefore, the university, and within it the ideal English school, must create a new common enterprise of understanding. It is the living language which both the university and its humane centre will explore and renew. The use of the language in studies of criticism will keep alive the continuous thread of cultural life. In *Education and the University*, in an appendix on 'Mass civilisation and minority culture', Leavis wrote of the 'very small minority' who are capable of benefiting from an ideal English school: 'In their keeping . . . is the language, the changing idioms, upon which fine living depends, and without which distinction of spirit is thwarted and incoherent' (Leavis 1943: 145).

William Walsh's (1980) critical study of Leavis reminds the reader that the theme of cultivation 'through that sensitive application to words' is consistent in Leavis' writing from before 1939 until his last collected writings. In a set of lectures in America published in his last years, again Leavis linked the two ideas, the university and the continuity and creativity of language. He reminded his audience of the inherent difficulty of talking, even to an highly educated group of listeners, and of being able to assume what is to be necessarily taken for granted:

> One can only be clear about one's focal interest and determine one's course and one's economy in relation to that. Mine – ours I may say – is the university; that is the function and the idea. (Leavis and Leavis 1969: 15)

Lord Snow, he told them, pressed us to acknowledge beauty and great human achievement in science:

> But there is a prior human achievement of collaborative creation, a more basic work of the mind of man (and more than the mind); one without which the triumphant creation of the scientific edifice would not have been possible: That is, the creation of the human world, including language. (Leavis and Leavis 1969: 16)

This achievement cannot, however, be left in the lap of history; it must be consciously and deliberately fostered. The place where the language can be consciously kept alive and, more than that, developed, is the university. What can we say of the relevance and value of this high calling and for Leavis' ideas as the century ends?

How best to learn: A language community

Language and the community that shares language is a good place to begin to make some critical and analytical points about Leavis' idea of an English school within an ideal university. Walsh points out how close this thesis is to Coleridge's conception of a living tradition. We shall find more parallels between Coleridge and Leavis as we progress, but, at this point, the crucial issue to notice is that language for *both* Coleridge and Leavis lives and changes in the abiding human groups and in the conservative institution of society. A strong English tradition is apparent here, namely the idea of an educational community. As we noticed in the chapter on Newman, this notion is of some significance in the ways that higher education institutions have been either maintained or renewed or developed in new settings in the UK, and it is a theme I shall return to in the conclusion to this book. In the specific context of the key texts we are now considering, the tradition of the community of learning can be traced from Coleridge through Newman, Matthew Arnold and T. S. Eliot to Leavis himself. However, he would have immediately rounded on any historian of ideas with the charge of missing the wood for the trees. That same tradition, as he was to argue powerfully in *The Great Tradition* (1948), was maintained in a living form, not in the works of social or theological thinkers, but in the living work of creative writers, particularly the great nineteenth-century novelists such as Jane Austen, George Eliot and Dickens and on into writers like Henry James, Joseph Conrad and D. H. Lawrence. They, he asserts, kept the flame alive, renewed it and interact with the reader through their use of the inherited language. Furthermore, they are 'public' thinkers because of the open accessible nature of the novel. The participants in the creative process of reading are from a much wider sphere than scholars or specialist critics. Great novelists are also 'incomparable students and critics of society and civilisation, and incomparable social historians' (Leavis 1943: 174). There is, in this view, no need for a specialist educational language. Learning is a shared, universal facility, not confined to universities, although the university is the only institution capable of assuming the responsibility of encouraging that living tradition.

Of all the writers in this collection of European thinkers who have considered the idea of the university, only Ortega y Gasset can present such a chilling scene as Leavis paints. He and Ortega can depict the forces that mass to obliterate the continuity of the European tradition and yet, at the same time, they can confidently demonstrate that there are agencies to oppose them. To Ortega, there are indeterminate, vital, even mysterious forces that may, in the course of history, effect change, despite the powers of the masses and particularly of the manipulated and manipulative press. Leavis has a bleaker view of the strength of the mass media. He encouraged in *Scrutiny* and in early educational works such as *Culture and Environment* (Leavis and Thompson 1933), a critical eye to be cast on the media, on advertising and on the general propaganda of politicians. Already, by 1933, these exercises seemed like a forlorn last-ditch stand. The argument for the university as the last bastion of resistance is a much more strongly argued and confident case than the general education programme of *Culture and Environment*. He is clearly a prophet with one basic message and, of course, prophets with one message are immediately dismissed as cranks or as narrow-minded. If 'narrow-mindedness' is the same as singleness of purpose, then Leavis' prophecy qualifies on grounds of unwavering determination and repetition of mission. His is a strongly moral argument about values in society, values in literature and values in the idea of a university. Leavis inevitably became increasingly alienated from the forces in the UK that encouraged a functional, utilitarian view of higher education, closely related to the material needs of society. His retort to the reformers was to brand them with Matthew Arnold's own term, 'Philistine'. The problem was, however, that the value-base that he defended became increasingly an inner circle of friends and students, using the same language of argument and admiring the same authors. It is important to examine first why Leavis and those who supported him established a minority group instead of a broader movement, although it was a powerful one in the teaching of English.

First, there is the charge of élitism to consider. This is not something from which Leavis himself ever sheltered. What he may not have realized was the force of egalitarianism and the demand for higher education that gathered momentum and was supported in strangely different but, in outcome, similar ways, by both left and right after the Second World War. This momentum gathered speed towards the student demonstrations of Western Europe and the USA in the late 1960s. Egalitarianism was irrelevant to Leavis' aim and foreign to his experience of teaching in a Cambridge college. Leavis is quite clear that the 'ancient universities' of Oxford and Cambridge have great potential as 'foci' of enormous influence. The character training that he details in chapter two of *Education and the University*, entitled 'A sketch for an English school', is appropriate in the setting of a Cambridge college. There, he states, the students were selected after a highly concentrated sixth-form career which, for the best of them, enabled a high level of starting point on which the university teacher built a style of learning which is largely self-driven. The 'prospecting and ranging mind' is prepared and selected before the ideal university process begins. In a letter to *The Times* in reply to Lord Annan, published as a final part of *English Literature in Our Time and the University*, Leavis states his position on the selection of the young student in terms which were at odds with the general opinion of university reformers and most politicians of the time of Lord Robbins' Report on Higher Education. He writes as follows: 'Only a limited proportion of any young adult group is capable of profiting by, or enjoying, university education' (Leavis 1967: 187).

Similarly, in an essay of 1947, he rejects notions of Cambridge as a regional university of East Anglia and adds, 'I am avowedly concerned with the training of an élite and my discussion postulates the appropriate material' (Singh 1986:

169). Unlike most of the other writers in this study, Leavis lived and worked through a period when the universities became more accessible to larger numbers of students. After the Second World War, the idea of equality of opportunity of education became not only a political ideal but also in a limited, but numerically considerable sense, a practical reality. In Great Britain in particular, the politics of university growth, and the corresponding diversification of higher education into a variety of institutions, occupied centre stage for the debate about higher education. I am not asserting that this process did not occur in the other countries of Western Europe, but there was a particular nexus of problems about the English and Welsh situation (and to a lesser extent, the Scottish) because of what had been previously a narrow concentration of institutions. Until 1960, higher education was concentrated in a small number of chartered institutions, with a particular domination by the two oldest universities. The fact that Leavis was a member of one of them, albeit, in his view, a mistrusted 'insider', makes the issue of the selection of ability particularly important in assessing his version of the ideal university.

One other 'local' feature, related to Leavis' educational experience, must be taken into account in weighing the importance of his clear stand in the training of an élite. This is his membership of a Cambridge college. Readers of Newman will find much to compare in his strong support for collegiate teaching. In the text of 1943, he had, with the stimulus of the University of Wisconsin experiment in mind, put forward his idea as an 'experiment' operating, we presume, in parallel with the traditional Tripos (examination) system of the University. In the 1947 essay referred to above, he develops his ideas a step further. He sees the constituent college of the University as the potential source for a new liberal education. It is the college, in fact, by which 'we can hope to save the University'. Readers should be aware that the college, in slightly different ways and in detail varying with the subjects studied, for both Oxford and Cambridge undergraduates is the locus of teaching. Crudely, the University organizes lectures, laboratories, etc., and the colleges 'tutor' or 'supervise' the students singly or in small groups. This form of teaching, as we have seen above, is the setting for the dialogue which Leavis envisages as the vehicle for his proposed new humane centre. The college is, therefore, even more than the university itself, 'a place set apart'. In Leavis' scheme, reform begins in true cell-like manner, with the small group, highly trained and sensitized by dialogue within a special language culture. Then, from this base, an élite – in the special sense of a selected refined band of reform – can spread outwards to save the university and then on to perpetuate the cultural tradition of Western civilization.

The identification of the collegiate teaching base for change and outward growth introduces the topic of dialogue. In many respects, Leavis makes an uncomfortable partner with some of the Western European thinkers here, but, in stressing the prime importance of the process of shared dialogue, he has much in common with Jaspers, Horkheimer and Tillich. Learning is not a solitary craft. Learning is not merely enhanced by teaching, it grows and develops by the dialogue of teacher and student, becoming something greater than anything an individual, however brilliant, could produce. Even the work of the most individual players in this scene, the novelists, poets and dramatists, who produce the texts for teacher and student, only have the appearance of being isolated and lonely. First, their work has been produced out of a shared community of discourse within the living cultural continuity of their own time. Second, their writings come alive from the printed page through the discussion between teacher and student. The method of teaching and learning envisaged by Leavis is, however, markedly different from the traditional Socratic procedure which, we have seen, Jaspers continues to admire. The literary-critical dialogue is a partnership of learning with a living language as a focus. In one important way, however, its end and achievement is not dissimilar to the German thinkers in this study. Like them, Leavis is not proposing a form of learning which exercises a level of rationality that absorbs only the intellect of the student. There is a higher level of learning which is both intellect and feeling, sensitivity and sense, which the tutor and student achieve together. This is why Leavis' own language is packed with key words such as 'creativity', 'consciousness' and 'spiritual climate', and his proposal is to satisfy, not curiosity or intellectual restlessness, but 'humanity's . . . profound and desperate need' (Leavis 1967: 31). Therefore Leavis places on the study of literature a grave burden. There is, in his dogma, 'no other access to anything approaching a full continuity of mind, spirit and sensibility – which is what we desperately need' (Leavis 1967: 60).

Like Newman and Jaspers, Leavis is arguing that higher learning is an activity of the whole human being. Like them also, he must face the bewilderment of critics who feel locked out from the proposed special community. For Leavis in particular, there was continuous difficulty created by the incomprehension of his many critics. In many ways, he had himself to blame, although many rejected his work with a cursory or second-hand reading. The most telling instance of this difficulty is in a characteristic statement or question of pedagogy, which he repeatedly uses to illustrate what should happen in an ideal exchange of tutor and student as literary critics. In *English Literature in our Time*, he asserts that critical judgements have the form 'This is so, isn't it?' Not only is this the master addressing the novice, it is, he is quick to add, a question which expects a response, such as 'Yes . . . but . . .'. The critical act demands collaboration of a fully overt kind, a 'many-sided real exchange'. It is not easy for many students of literature, never mind for people working in other unrelated academic disciplines, to accept the leadership implied in 'This is so . . . isn't it?', no matter how much that question becomes more genuine because a collaborative response is needed. The dilemma is self-generated. English literary criticism is an acquired discipline, and those who have been through that process became sensitive to the nature of literature and to a wider and wider sphere of human culture, but it is a sensitivity only acquired by the process of guided reading. The process is not easy to communicate to the uninitiated in the way that, say, a historian or a physicist might explain their methods of exploration and their choice of activities. Almost immediately after publication of the first issues of *Scrutiny*, the opprobrium of 'selectivity' and 'criteria' became attached to the contributers and, eventually, to their students. Group terms, such as 'Leavisites' and 'Scrutineers' were applied liberally. On the one hand, this labelling process gave an impetus of co-ordination to a loosely gathered group, both inside and outside Cambridge, but it also implied the formation of a committed movement or party. Instead of a central English school, dispensing sweetness and light in the ideal university, the very opposite appeared to be formed: a critical group of disciples with their own journal at times embattled against the academic establishment. The Leavis 'school' acquired a pejorative meaning. Ironically, the experimental school he had actually proposed never took place. In practice, the 'Leavisites' became increasingly peripheral rather than central to the university in which it had its birth and on which its founder had placed such a weight of confidence.

The last point should be qualified in two ways, both of which have an indirect bearing on the nature of the university in post-war Western Europe. Leavis' critical work, much more than his directly educational writings, could never be said to be on the periphery of studies in English literature in the world at large. His work was, undoubtedly, one of the foremost academic 'exports' of post-war Britain, particularly to the USA, whose influence on Europe he was to deplore so openly. A sequence of students and colleagues directly taught by him spread widely in departments of English literature and education in universities at home and overseas. The wide-ranging nature of the articles in *Scrutiny* may have indirectly prepared the ground for the outspoken social criticism of industrial society common in some education circles. The deep suspicion of the develop-ment of affluence could be observed in the UK in the 1960s and 1970s at least. Many of the most trenchant critics of modern life are unlikely to have read the *Scrutiny* articles directly, but they had often been influenced by schoolteachers, themselves tutored by Leavis or by his senior collaborators. The second, related area of influence was on the schools and teacher training colleges, or, at least, the English departments of those institutions. Denys Thompson, an early collabor-ator with Leavis on a text intended for younger students, *Culture and Environment* (1933), was to publish for many years a very influential journal, later called *The Use of English*, which was supported directly by secondary schoolteachers and by training college lecturers.

The English teacher-training system had been one of the first areas to receive the barbs of *Scrutiny*, in an article by L. C. Knights (1932). In the crucial period of the expansion of teacher training in England and Wales from 1952 to 1972, the 'main subject' area (as it was called for most of that period) of English was, it must be remembered, in a close relationship with university departments of English. They in their turn had a sprinkling of those who had been influenced by Leavis. Furthermore, the literary figures in the 'Great Tradition', particularly the very accessible novelists such as Jane Austen, George Eliot, Charles Dickens, Joseph Conrad and, perhaps above all, D. H. Lawrence, were felt to be singularly appropriate figures for study by intending teachers. For one thing, their work gave an entry into the social background of their period. For different, more complex reasons, there was an apparent harmony with parallel educational notions. Think, for instance, of the support of 'integration' of subject areas of the school curriculum chiefly in primary and some state secondary schools. The breaking of barriers between subject disciplines and the study of issues and topics involving the interaction of disciplines were prominent features of the British eduction scene before the advent of the National Curriculum in 1989. The two Leavises and Denys Thompson seemed to be stating the same thesis, of the cohesion of life and the wholeness of experience. Literature provided an accessible key to this form of social understanding. In addition, the strong sense of moral seriousness underlying *Scrutiny's* judgements of literature or the almost puritanical attack on the advance of the mass society, on advertising agencies and on the irresponsible press, were all in tune with the strong forces supporting social responsibility of the profession of teaching. The very popular and widely distributed texts by Richard Hoggart (*The Uses of Literacy*, 1957) and Raymond Williams (*The Long Revolution*, 1964), appeared to share the same sense of the decline of older, rooted standards, to which *Culture and the Environment* or articles in *Scrutiny* or *The Use of English* regularly contributed evidence. A whiff of nostalgia pervaded some very different and oddly assorted intellectual partners in this period; nevertheless, it cannot be denied that Leavis' major influence was, ironically, less in the universities than in institutions which a decade after his death were to be part of the very outcome he most deplored: the rapid proliferation of more centres of higher education, based for the most part on the accumulation of courses and disciplines with no 'humane centre' to act as a coherent force. The colleges which had been a sympathetic environment for the messages from *Scrutiny* 'diversified', as the jargon had it, and aimed for size and variety rather than for wholeness and unity.

Why did the idea of a school within the university fail?

The reasons for Leavis' apparent failure to establish a genuine educational experiment in his own centre of learning are both local or personal and structural. The personal reasons for his lack of a base to exercise influence in Cambridge need not detain the reader here. They are well recorded, and in a sympathetic manner by Walsh (1980). What is more important for the thesis of this work is to examine the reasons for the failure to establish a university with one particular discipline as the combining and common centre. Mulhern, from a Marxist viewpoint, makes a trenchant criticism not only of Leavis but of the discipline he represents:

> 'Literary criticism' as it is mainly practised in England is in reality the focal activity of a discourse whose foremost general cultural function is the repression of politics . . . (this discourse has done much) to shape, and still sustains, England's cultivated, politically philistine (and so conformist) intelligentsia. (Mulhern 1979: 331)

In brief, in this view, English was doomed from the start as a radical device for changing anything, particularly the oldest educational institutions. Strangely enough, Leavis himself would have agreed with the dismissal of the same 'intelligentsia'. The finer life of the cultural tradition, he pointed out, in the preface of the second edition of *Education and the University*, is a very different matter 'from being given over to insert traditionalism, academic gentility and museum conservation of the forms of past life' (Leavis 1943: 11).

Without accepting Mulhern's direct point, it is possible to agree that the underestimation of where the power to change the university lay was the gravest defect in this proposal to reform a university's system from a single discipline 'centre'. Leavis was working against the tide, which strongly ran in favour of science and technology. Gradually, as was demonstrated during the late 1970s and early 1980s, the political (rather than necessarily the scholarly) importance of the physical, technological and economic sciences increased at least in the eyes of those who paid the piper if not always of those who played the tune. Historians of the rise and fall of the curriculum might add a footnote on the advance of the social sciences in this period. Leavis' concept of English studies in *Scrutiny* and elsewhere appeared to be inclusive of many of the areas of concern of social scientists: the state of culture obviously, but also social trends, the quality of urban life and the rapid changes of rural life. One major defect in the proposition of English as a focus for a socially conscious curriculum was that, to the social scientists it selected a particular view of society (see, for instance, Lepenies 1988). To these in other fields, Leavis claimed too much territory.

A further defect with English studies as a unifying centre was the acceleration of disintegrating forces within English departments themselves. Leavis, of course, could not have known the scale of dissension and division within the humanities and social sciences from 1970 onwards. It is not hard, for instance, to imagine what Leavis' response would have been to the following quotation from a general editor of a widely used series of texts entitled *New Accents*. Terence Hawkes confidently asserts that this is a time of rapid social change.

> Yet this is nowhere more apparent than in the central field of what may, in general terms, be called literary studies. Here, among large numbers of students at all levels of education, the erosion of the assumptions and presuppositions that support the literary disciplines in their conventional form has proved fundamental modes and categories inherited from the past no longer seem to fit the reality experienced by a new generation. (Elam 1980: ix)

This was a phenomenon not confined to English studies; it was felt above all in history and sociology and in the study of the arts. In the period from 1968 onwards (with its roots much earlier of course), the traditional homogeneity of the so-called 'arts subjects' was broken and the division of left and right, of structuralism and post-structuralism, of modernism and post-modernism (the labels proliferated every five years), made a 'common humane centre' impossible to believe in. The university world had been transformed from without and from within into a new plural 'polis' and the moment for Leavis' English school had been lost.

One final point may be made before closing with my judgement of the inherent value of his message. Leavis was engaged, at least in the 1930s, in reaching for a solution to what may be a peculiarly English preoccupation, the demise of classical learning. A marked feature of the university system in England, and to a lesser degree in Scotland, for the majority of the nineteenth century and at least until the 1920s, was the domination in terms of prestige of classics as a university study. It could be argued that the range of disciplines studied by undergraduates, at least at Oxford and Cambridge, had become less diverse as the universities increased the rigour of the undergraduate courses. Compare, for instance, the range of work at St John's College, Cambridge followed by the poet William Wordsworth, not a leading undergraduate in academic achievement, from 1787 to 1791 (mathematics including Newton, moral philosophy and classics) (see Schneider 1957), with the curriculum of 'Greats' firmly and securely established in Oxford in mid-century. The point is that 'Greats' was considered to be a total education in itself, covering philosophy, history and language, but in prestige terms it was a continuing and fairly unchanging sector of power in the two dominant universities. Undoubtedly, the contributing factor which helped to sustain classical learning as the 'humane centre' of the two ancient universities was the equally dominant position of political and ecclesiastical leaders of the nation, who had themselves been educated in this tradition. Perhaps the very security, stability and continuity of Victorian England, compared with the political turbulence of Western Europe, helped to preserve, well into the twentieth century, the idea of a 'centre' of humane studies within a university's curriculum. Classical learning continued to be accepted as a discipline for training for leadership and character. It had an influence on the selection of the curriculum followed by other studies gathering around it, for example on the study of English literature. It was, in the twentieth century, rapidly losing ground and no longer could claim to be a 'centre', and it is plain from Leavis' own accounts, as well as from other writings of the inter-war years, that there was an urgency to 'fill the gap' left by the decline of classical learning. Therefore, in the text of 1943 discussed above, Leavis used the language that the defenders of the classics themselves would have understood. His own phrases are equally applicable to classical studies: the training of 'a central intelligence', 'informed general intelligence', 'humane culture', 'a sense of value informed by a traditional wisdom', 'the finest experience of the human experience of the past', and so on. This is not to say that Leavis is ignorant of the complex processes that had accelerated the decay of classical learning. He reminds us that the ideal of a subject which claimed to equip the man or woman of the future to be a Renaissance scholar, was impossible in the twentieth century. The empty space was, however, there to be seized and an English school could occupy it. What he found difficult to see was that the political and educational consensus that over many decades had permitted that central space to exist for classics no longer existed. The common ground was not available for any discipline.

What remains of value?

Two important presumptions held by Leavis remain for consideration by those who discuss and plan the universities and colleges of the future. One is so central to all the discussions of writers in this book that it can be reserved for the conclusion and therefore should not detain us for long at this particular point. It is the social function of the university. What exactly is the 'third realm' to use his phrase? Does it reside in one university, in the universities as a group or is it a dispersed influence? Is a new humanely educated English intelligentsia likely to be of more effective worth than the urbane variety that Leavis frequently castigates? The diagnosis of the 'modern predicament' has not changed since Leavis so urgently defined it, although its formulation differs from writer to writer as the generations pass. The role of the press (and largely post-Leavis, the visual media), the advance of 'Philistinism' and 'technologico-Benthamism', defined variously as it may be from left and right, are not less but more dominant. What still hovers on the agenda is whether higher education should be constructed to oppose these forces. Is the university or college an active agent for transforming society or are they providers of highly trained functionaries and technologists to make the public machine run well? Leavis' questions and his bold solution that the university is the special place of opposition still remain on the table for discussion.

Perhaps the chief significance of Leavis' educational work is hidden from the cursory reader and may indeed have surprised Leavis himself. He turns out to be a major supporter of the power of continuous, historical institutions. It is easy to identify a non-institutional Leavisite influence, as we have seen above, in a dispersed 'movement' across school classrooms, college tutorials, publishing houses, and indeed in creative writers' workshops. At heart, however, Leavis' own message of 1943 is that the historic institution, the university (and one particular university), is the continuous centre of value. He is essentially traditionalist in institutional terms as well as in terms of the continuity of literature. 'Our business', he said in 1967, 'our vital need is to maintain the continuity of life and consciousness that a cultural tradition is, and not to lose anything essential from our heritage' (Leavis 1967: 183). The institution that carries this awesome responsibility of heritage is not a journal or a political movement, but the university. Burke or Coleridge would not have demurred from the sentiments of the quotation, although the first would have put the responsibility into Parliament and the second into the Church or his ideal version of it. We owe to Leavis a debt for speaking in favour of the university from a critical position within that institution. His was an unswerving loyalty, despite the fact that some of his most trenchant criticism was directed at university teachers. His success in creating a movement and indeed his own criticisms of academic establishments have obscured this basic conservative element in his education thinking. Ultimately universities matter.

References

Elam, K. (1980). *The Semiotics of Theatre and Drama*. London, Methuen.

Eliot, T. S. (1932). *Selected Essays*. London, Faber and Faber.

Eliot, T. S. (1939). *The Idea of a Christian Society*. London, Faber and Faber.

Hoggart, R. (1957). *The Uses of Literacy*. London, Chatto and Windus.

Knights, L. C. (1932). Will Training Colleges bear Scrutiny? *Scrutiny*, December.

Leavis, F. R. (1934). Why universities? *Scrutiny*, September.

Leavis, F. R. (1943). *Education and the University: A Sketch for an 'English School'*. Cambridge, Cambridge University Press (2nd edition, 1979).

Leavis, F. R. (1948). *The Great Tradition*, London, Chatto and Windus.

Leavis, F. R. (1963). *'Scrutiny': A Retrospect*. Cambridge, Cambridge University Press.

Leavis, F. R. (1967). *English Literature in Our Time and the University: The Clark Lectures*. Cambridge, Cambridge University Press.

Leavis, F. R. and Leavis, Q. D. (1969). *Lectures in America*. New York, Pantheon.

Leavis, F. R. and Thompson, D. (1933). *Culture and Environment: The Training of Critical Awareness*. London, Chatto and Windus.

Lepenies, W. (1988). *Between Literature and Science: The Rise of Sociology*. Cambridge, Cambridge University Press.

Mulhern, F. (1979). *The Moment of 'Scrutiny'*. London, New Left Books.

Schneider, B. R. (1957). *Wordsworth's Cambridge Education*. Cambridge, Cambridge University Press.

Singh, G. (Ed.) (1986). *F. R. Leavis: Valuations in Criticisms and Other Essays*. Cambridge, Cambridge University Press.

Walsh, W. (1980). *F. R. Leavis*. London, Chatto and Windus.

Williams, R. (1961). *The Long Revolution*. London, Chatto and Windus.

7

Paul Tillich: Learning and Living with 'Profundity and Paradox'

In Paul Tillich we have a writer who presents us with a dilemma; he could be said to offer too much information about knowledge. On the other hand, his willingness to write about his own life as a scholar, frequently as an introduction to a theological disquisition, gives us useful material. It is not only that he is a prolific writer, but students and fellow theologians who came under his spell write about him at length. What has not been done in any systematic way is to extract from the mass of material a clear doctrine of what he would say a good university is or might be. In short, there is no one text such as Jaspers or Ortega provided. Furthermore, his introspective autobiographical material is thick with information, but much of it was repeated in other texts and there is a working over of perennial themes. There is some evidence, as we shall see, that Tillich conveys an unoriginal view of learning, in that other thinkers were saying similar things at the same time, although his ideas are in an original personal dress. His thinking on education is none the worse for being part of a contemporary climate of thought and it has the virtue of being individually documented. Indeed, individualism could be said to be the quintessentially Tillichian 'method'. The task is therefore to tease out individual emphases rather than original lines and new departures.

The most accessible autobiographical sources are in a series of lectures given at the Chicago University Law School towards the end of his life (Tillich 1967) and in a pre-war work, *The Interpretation of History* (Tillich 1936). In both works, the same autobiographical experiences are worked over, namely his early childhood and his years as an undergraduate. In the analysis of his ideas in the following paragraphs, I shall chiefly refer to both texts with other glimpses of his early life. In only one passing reference does he provide us with 'an ideal university'. Let us briefly consider that reference before moving on to what are more interesting key texts.

In the autobiographical sketch called 'On the boundary' (Tillich 1936), Tillich tells us that, in the period of reconstruction after 1918, he actually submitted a plan for a university's curriculum. His criticism of the older curriculum, familiar to readers of Jaspers, is that the old humanistic ideal of classicalism had been 'destroyed by the specialisation of sciences and by the increasing quantitative demands of professional training' (Tillich 1936: 21). In its place, he proposed a two-part curricular structure, very similar to the two-fold system of Ortega:

1. A set of professional schools.
2. A 'humanistic Faculty' representing 'the old humanistic ideal'.

This structure, again familiar to those who persisted with the chapter or Horkheimer, relies on the controlling influence of a civilizing, unifying core of the curriculum, in Horkheimer's case social philosophy. In Tillich's proposal, the unifier is to be a principle of learning rather than a single discipline. The humanistic faculty is to be 'ruled by a philosophy which, according to the original idea of philosophy, was to discover the question of our human existence by means of the Logos' (Tillich 1936: 22). The practical proposal need not occupy our attention any longer. It never came to fruition. Two points emerge from it though that are worthy of note: first, that the university is a socially engaged, responsible, institution (or a border, in a 'battlefield') and, secondly, that the action of philosophy is through the word (Logos). To the second point we shall return in due course.

The key text: How Tillich was taught and what he learned

The real 'key text' is a much less obvious piece of autobiographical writing and, perhaps for that reason, a less guarded, less edited source. Slight though it is, it is a source capable of leading us into much more interesting considerations of Tillich's contributions to the idea of the moulding of the intellectual. In 1943, Thomas Mann, preparing in Switzerland to write his great novel *Dr Faustus*, was to write to Tillich for background material. Mann wanted to know what had been the pre-1914 education of the theologian in Germany. Tillich's reply is illuminating (Lyons 1969). He compares liberal theology with conservative theology:

> It seemed to us that they [liberal theologians] lacked insight into the 'daemonic' character of human existence. . . . We concluded that the conservative tradition had preserved more of the true understanding of human nature and of the tragedy of human existence than had the liberal progressive bourgeois ideology. Already at that time Kierkegaard was exercising a strong influence on a small group of theological students at Halle. In our view liberal theology lacked profundity and paradox and I am convinced that world history has proved our view correct. (Lyons 1969: 104)

With the hindsight of 1943, world history had demonstrated that the 'demonic' and the tragic were all too visible. He continued in this letter to Thomas Mann as follows:

> In response to your question regarding the cultural affirmation of liberal theology, I can only say that it did indeed represent a far-reaching

adaptation to the ideals of bourgeois society, above all by emphasising as strongly as possible the ethically based personality ideal. Religiosity became, so to speak, a function of humanness, measured by the yardstick of the developing human personality. The ecstatic and paradoxical aspects of the religious were reduced to an ethical Faith in progress. (Lyons 1969: 105)

The ideals of a bourgeois society were concerned with other ends, and therefore an important dimension of religion had withered for many at the expense of the rapid, apparently confident march of human progress. These criticisms give us a clue to Tillich's consistently held convictions about the nature of learning in any highest or, as he would say, deepest sense. Profundity and ecstasy, paradox and ambiguity are the true nature of intellectual pursuits. Reassuring consolation or assurances of inevitable perfection and resolution are false fruits.

The letter to Thomas Mann also contains a revealing comment on one of Tillich's teachers. We shall return later in this chapter to the importance of the experience of teaching and learning for this writer.

All others seemed minor to us when compared to the stature of this man Kaehler. We attended his lectures not because of the systematic theology he taught rather drily and from a text-book but for the sake of what as students we referred to as 'fringe benefits', namely, his interpolations which influenced all of us profoundly throughout our maturity. My friends and I owe to him the realization that our thinking also is broken and requires 'justification' and that dogmatism is consequently the intellectual analog of phariseeism. (Lyons 1969: 103–4)

In order to pursue these ideas further, we shall consider in turn the notion of the essential dilemmas of education and the teaching relationship, his view of the ecstatic nature of reason linked with how humanity learns and, finally, why people are impelled to learn at all.

The dilemmas of education: The nature of humanity

Tillich sees that formal education poses a special problem for anyone who believes in the necessity of individual choice. Educating someone may result in reducing that person's freedom to choose. The process of improvement of a learner may be fraught with risks to freedom. Let us see how this is argued.

The most extreme political systems, to give a clear but extreme illustration, use a process called 'education' for controlling people. Under such a system, education is organized by the powerful to have the most direct influences on the taught, restricting their vision to that of the teacher/leader. In one form of totalitarian society, for instance, the educational system attempts to adjust the learner to the demands of a system of production and consumption. Even in non-totalitarian societies, he argues in *Theology of Culture* (Tillich 1964), education can be based on presumptions that the learner is first and foremost a consumer and agent of society. Tillich explains that this process/production model of education arises from a naive belief in human perfectibility, for, as belief in the Kingdom of God declined, belief in peace and justice through the process of history was substituted. A view that men and women could be made into perfect elements in an improved society is, he argues, a natural consequence of the elimination of the divine. However, not only the divine, but also the 'demonic' disappeared and, in their place, was substituted a simplistic definition of humanity. Appropriately, a simplistic model of the person as learner was produced and passive reception of preordained learning was desired. The terrible consequences of passivity, assumed by the powerful and accepted by the weak, are drawn to our attention by Tillich as by many others of his generation. For Tillich, the notion of the learner as a receptive vessel is dangerous, not only because it pretends to have eradicated the demonic in life, but it is also undesirable because it is also a reduction of humanity's power to engage with learning in a fully human way. Here we reach a nub of thought. To surrender a human faculty, in this case the capacity to engage with learning, is deeply offensive to the existentialist thinker. In contrast, the existentialist thinker faces up to his or her active part in learning. He or she is 'the interested or passionate thinker' (Tillich 1964: 89) not the objective receiver. Concurrently, the 'passionate thinker' must live with tragic knowledge, rather than with a false sense of security that modern life has eradicated risk.

Another paradoxical aspect of education is raised by the issues of subjectivity and objectivity. The two terms 'subject' and 'object' occupy an important part of Tillich's major life-work, *Systematic Theology* (Tillich 1968). The detail of this polarity need not delay us here, except to use the two terms in the way Tillich uses them to illustrate what he takes to be a further essential dilemma of education. The subject (a person) is changed and able to achieve personal self-creation only by the effect of the action of other people. However, a deliberately planned action, which we call education, impinging on a subject, almost inevitably destroys that subject, because the subject changes over into its opposite, an object: 'Working towards the growth of a person is at the same time working towards his de-personalisation. Trying to enhance a subject makes it an object' (Tillich 1968: vol. III, 80).

The two educational extremes, totalitarian indoctrination braced by discipline and liberal unconcern accompanied by permissiveness, both have disastrous effects on the individual as an individual. The first objectifies the subject; the second leaves the student 'alone in bondage to himself'. Both tendencies may be found in schools and colleges, even in the less extreme forms of the educational system. The very process of setting out to change a subject leads the educator into the heart of the dilemma of depersonalization, no matter how much the teacher attempts to respect the independence of the learner.

A further in-built dilemma for the educator who wishes to leave his or her student free is contained in a traditional objective of a humanist education, which is commonly said to be one of bringing out what is innate or of actualizing human potential. How, asks Tillich, can something as general as human potential be actualized within one person when at the same time we claim a unique individuality for that person? Education must therefore really mean the actualization of 'all human potential in terms of the historical destiny of a particular individual'. More serious still for unnerving the modern educator, is Tillich's opinion that not all individuals are likely to benefit from an educational process which seeks to develop full human potential: 'Whether under aristocratic or democratic systems, the vast majority of human beings (are excluded) from the higher grades of cultural form and educational depth' (Tillich 1968: vol. III, 9).

We shall leave consideration of this élitist judgement until later, but there is to Tillich one further deficiency of education *per se*. It is that education pretends to resolve ambiguities and to lead to clarity and resolution. In fact, in terms of humanistic education, it is over-clarified, it fails to include the full story of human existence. It resolves away what Tillich calls 'the ambiguities of the law', or rather the in-built ambiguity of life itself. In a humanistic education, without the insights of religion, education is not equipped to initiate people into 'the mystery of being'. Instead, 'secular education has to initiate learners into the needs of a society whose needs and ends remain finite in spite of their endlessness' (Tillich 1968: vol. III, 107). Education in humanistic context presumes, in other words, a predictability and an order in the world. In fact, there is no such certainty. A religiously informed education will not fare better if it too is based on certain lies and unambiguous messages. Religion (or rather true religion) is founded on a different premise. Life is, in truth, paradoxical and ambiguous. The function of both education and religion is not to smooth away these wrinkles, but to open eyes to see them. Much of modern education, therefore, is based on clarity and firm guidance about what can never be clear and certain. As such, education is false and doomed.

All is not total gloom (although Tillich could easily serve as a basic model of a conservative, even pessimistic, educational thinker). There is a positive way or rather a positive attitude that the good educator might adopt. The sensitive teacher must allow the learner, the 'centred person', to be directed to ultimate matters 'from which he receives independence without internal chaos' (Tillich 1968: vol. III, 27). In the best form of teaching, subject and object are 'fragmentarily conquered and humanity is fragmentarily achieved' (ibid.: 27). We are to consider all education, and higher education in particular, as provisional in its achievement. The place of learning is a sensitive plot where imposed circumstances and conditions will destroy the very plant they set out to nurture. Education is therefore always *in via*, always travelling in hope and with a belief in potential being, never fully and never finally, but always occasionally, released. When that moment on a continuous journey is reached, it is a time of great excitement and joy.

Tillich, reason and the way people learn

Much of the argument of the previous paragraphs will beg the question, 'What does Tillich believe happens in the process of learning, what is his psychological theory?' To understand this aspect of this thinking, we have to turn to his definition of reason or rather his definitions of reason, since he makes not one but a number of distinctions between what he sees as different ways that humanity applies reasoning powers. As Martin (1963: 37) says, 'To no single topic in the doctrine of man does Tillich give more serious and sustained attention than to the nature and limits of human rationality.' The main source of his thinking on this matter is set out at length in volume 1 of *Systematic Theology* (Tillich 1968), but it is possible to grasp fairly quickly one important distinction between two main types of reason. In my view, it is a dichotomy which at least might cause someone engaged in higher education to pause and to reconsider previously held assumptions about learning.

In *Systematic Theology*, Tillich posits that the first type of reason is *technical* (or formal) reason, which is narrow, reduced to a capacity for logical analysis and similar functions. The second type, *ontological* reason, is wide in its embrace. It includes the cognitive and the aesthetic, the theoretical and the practical. It is detached as well as passionate, subjective at the same time as it is objective. In classical thinking, this second type of reason was considered to be the structure of the mind which not only grasped but transformed reality. Tillich argues that the two kinds of reason can work together in harmony, but there is a serious consequence if technical reason is separated and acts alone. In an educational context, when such separation occurs, technical reason will pursue some very threatening ends. Because technical reason acquires its ends from 'somewhere else', these may be provided by non-rational forces, either by positive traditions or by arbitrary decision serving the will to power (Tillich 1968: vol. I, 81). The intellectual separation of the two types has a diminishing effect on ontological reason also. Dimensions of ontological reason, such as eros and passion, are categorized by the educationalist who has separated the two forms as 'non-reason' and consigned them to the 'irrelevance of the subjectivity'. As I hope to illustrate in the summary of this chapter, there is much food for thought for the educator in these ideas, particularly in considering how various disciplines of the curriculum are first categorized, then allocated a position in a public hierarchy of priorities.

In an 'ideal type' of thinking, Tillich claims, both types of reason are in fact united. It is not always very clear how Tillich understood how this combined 'reason-in-unity' would work. Are there in fact two distinct types, as it were, brought together to create harmony, or is it nearer the truth to say that modern language conventionally separates the terms? Has modern life reached such a dire division that we are forced to perceive distinction where none needs exist? Tillich's psychological explanation is highly individual and, as with most of his writing, so much part of an elaborated system that it is not easy to select a passage that can explain his theory of reason and, at the same time, apply it readily to education as one element among others of human activity. It is, however, possible to see that his explanation of knowledge is derived from his own analysis of reason.

His logic is that, as there are different levels of reasoning from the narrow and formal to the wide, rich and all-embracing, so there are different levels of knowing. Much of volume III of *Systematic Theology*, as the title of one of its parts ('Life and spirit') indicates, is concerned with a deeper level than merely formal knowledge transactions. He tackles the question of how 'psychological material', which is 'always there', is transformed into knowledge. The essential step is the full involvement of the human being and particularly that being's 'personal centre'. This is essentially a philosophy of human engagement. It could easily be identified as the extreme opposite of the view of a human being that reduces him or her to a cipher, to a programmed, engineered item in a world master plan. The very act of cognition is the result of 'the transcendence of the [personal] centre over the psychological material' (Tillich 1968: vol. III, 32). The 'act of cognition' in this sense is obviously throbbing with significance far beyond the simple business of 'knowing' something. Of course, this is not the way cognition is usually discussed in psychological discourse. This is the language appropriate for a different kind of knowing, to which Tillich applies a high level of language:

> Such an act is the manifestation of the spirit. (Tillich 1968: vol. II, 32)
> Only the spirit can transcend the subject and object in education and guidance. (ibid.: 226)

In effect, this psychological process is closer to the traditional language of revelation rather than to discourse about knowledge. It is not surprising, therefore, to find that Tillich's own term for the heightened state of cognitive activity is 'ecstatic reason'. Martin traces similar descriptions by other theologians (such as Rudolf Otto's 'The ontological shock' in his *The Idea of the Holy*). We have seen in Jaspers' work a high-level state of knowing, which he called 'responsive reason'. Tillich's state of high-level perception, of some importance for studies at university level, is very similar to Jasper's conception. Whatever the origins and intellectual connections of Tillich's theory of knowledge, at this point we should perceive the semi-mystical language and take note that learning, although it is tough, demanding and even doomed, is an activity of excitement and deep self-fulfilment. Before losing our way in heavy stuff like this, let the balance be restored by listening to one further aspect of Tillich which relates to the activity of learning, namely the boundary situations of human existence.

We have seen that Tillich belongs to that group of philosophers who concentrate on the limitations of human possibility at the same time as seeking the action that can transcend limitations. It is important to remember that, despite all its talk of transcendence and possibility, it is not necessarily an optimistic world view; on the contrary, it rests on a form of the doctrine of the Fall. Nevertheless, it is a view which seeks out optimistic ends, for which it requires a belief in possibility. Furthermore, it suggests there is a human urge, a 'passionate longing for ultimate reality' (Tillich 1964: 8). We shall see when we look at the writing of Miguel de Unamuno that, like Tillich, he too built a philosophy on human finitude. A similar note was sounded in the chapters on Ortega and Karl Jaspers. What is of interest to the reader with an interest in education is how Tillich takes a different route from them to arrive at the concept of transcendence. It is through the notion of boundaries that Tillich proposes the way to break out of the iron circles of time and space.

Significantly and typically, it is from the experience of his own life that Tillich draws out the essential nature of the human frontiers. In *The Interpretation of History* (Tillich 1936), the autobiographical sketch begins with a chapter entitled 'On the boundary'. He describes how his childhood was in tension between city and country, between social classes, between reality and imagination, and so on. Similarly, as a young scholar, he was involved in the reconstruction of German universities which themselves stood between old and new. In the political turmoil of Germany in the early 1930s, he found himself like many other scholars on a frontier between contemplation and action, between standing back and becoming involved. In the event he was to be exiled, and so he escaped from this dangerous knife edge, only to experience the tension of belonging and not belonging to an adopted country.

> The border between theory and practice has become a battlefield, on which the fate of the university to come, and therewith of humanistic culture in the civilised world will be decided. (Tillich 1936: 22)

Like Sartre, a few years later at the beginning of the Second World War, the existentialist finds the true source of authenticity in personal experience (Sartre 1984). In Tillich's case, life on the frontier justified a whole schema of boundaries that he lists in the first part of *The Interpretation of History*. The quotation that follows is strongly reminiscent of Ortega and of Jaspers:

> To stand on many border lines means to experience in many forms the unrest, insecurity and inner limitation of existence and to know the inability of attaining serenity, security and perfection. (Tillich 1936: 72)

Whereas we could directly relate Jaspers' *Grenzensituationen* to the overlapping of the curriculum or to the points where different subject disciplines meet, Tillich's exploration of boundaries is more diffuse and much less easy to relate to issues such as the curriculum of higher education. Tillich appears almost deliberately to be seeking the conjunction of antitheses and courting the exchanges of opposites. As so many of his works demonstrate, particularly the popular collections of theology like *Theology of Culture* (1964) or *The Shaking of the Foundations* (1962), Tillich urges us to look deeper and deeper into experience. The starting point can be at any point of human experience persistently pursued; or rather traced to its depth, it will become a theological pursuit. So much is appropriate for the theologian of everyday experience. What is there to glean for the educationalist, acting as a professional specialist in the study of experience? Two directions are evident in a number of Tillich's works; one is the respect for knowledge (or rather 'true knowledge'), and the other is the familiar one of the philosopher drawing on his own life – in short the lived experience of being a scholar.

In previous paragraphs, we have discussed Tillich's highly individual explanation of a special, maximum form of ratiocination, of 'ecstatic reason'. We have no reason to labour the points already made about the attainment of this high plateau where knowledge is truly experienced. One important point remains. It is that Tillich, in any list of human priorities, puts the quest for knowledge at a superior level of human endeavour. Like others of his time, his explanation of why human beings have the urge to know is transcendental.

> Ultimate concern is manifest in the realm of knowledge as the passionate longing for ultimate reality. (Tillich 1964: 8)

> [To study is to] . . . act towards something beyond his depth. (ibid.: 31)

Not only is the quest for knowledge driven by a force which impels the scholar, it is also motivated by a pleasure principle. No mere curiosity this! Tillich writes about learning as if it is a form of thrilling experience. Again, his autobiographical information is the source of his argument. In the late work *My Search for Absolutes* (Tillich 1967), there is a long section describing this personal intellectual pilgrimage. His own student days and, later, the experiences at the zenith of his academic achievement in exile in the USA, confirmed for him in two different forms the importance of learning in a community.

In the 'key text' letter to Thomas Mann, Tillich writes with warmth of the 'hidden curriculum' of his student days:

> It might be of interest for your project to know that I belonged to the Christian Student Organization called 'Wingolf' and that the summer of 1907, when I was the 'First Officer' of this seventy-man group, seems to me even today yet to have been the greatest chapter of my life. Whatever I have become in a theological, philosophical, and human sense I owe only in part to the professors but contrariwise in an overwhelming measure to that organization whose theological and philosophical debates after midnight and the ensuring personal conversations before sunrise became decisive for my entire life. Music played a large part in all this. And the romantic relationship to nature, which in all my current class lectures I place in deliberate contrast to the Calvinistic-American estrangement from nature, I owe in the first instance to my trip at that time through Thuringia and to the Wartburg in the company of my fraternals. (Lyons 1969: 106)

Before 1914, therefore, he remembered that his inner life found sustenance not in a relationship with his tutors, the professors, but in the student Christian group which he commended as 'the first after the family'. Later he remembered again that this student group provided 'Communion, friendship, seriousness about the problems of communal life generally and Christian communal life especially' (Tillich 1967: 38). However, in the post-Hitler period of reconstruction, Tillich was to view the revival of German university fraternities with scepticism. Sojourns at US universities, particularly the Union Theological Seminary in New York, revealed to him a more inclusive academic community with scholars, professors, students and families mixing and meeting in halls, elevators, lectures, religious services and social gatherings: 'A counteraction against the extreme individualism of one's academic existence in Germany' (Tillich 1967: 47).

The wider academic community gave its members a wider experience of the tumultuous canvas of the century. The world's scholars, who passed through the Union Theological College seminary, were all in one sense or another engaged either as victims or as actors in history:

> We are not scholars according to the pattern of our teachers at the end of the nineteenth century. We were forced into history which made the analysis of history and of its contents most difficult. (Tillich 1967: 64)

The academic community and its complex interrelationships was one of the values he acquired from his own experience. His own pedagogic method is another indicator of the personal values of learning. Testified to by the writings of his friends and students as well as by his own introspective musings, there is much evidence of his dynamic teaching ability. A considerable part of his work started life in lectures or in seminars. Tillich was an inspired teacher who enjoyed company rather than the life of the lonely scholar. The shape and structure of his books bear witness to their origins in the lecture rooms of Europe and the USA. Former students recall the powerful way in which he taught (see, for instance, May 1974; Pauck and Pauck 1977: vol. 1), but there is even more revealing material in the autobiographical sources already referred to. In one account, Tillich himself uses a metaphor of how he worked, studied and wrote. In *My Search for Absolutes*, he claims to have used his lectures as 'decisive steps in my cognitive road' and then says that this teaching was 'like screws drilling into untouched rock' (Tillich 1967: 44). This particular route in the search for truth was effective for him because of the personality of the persons engaged in dialogue. Such a view is consistent with 'existential truth, this is to say a truth which lives in the immediate self-expression of an experience' (Tillich 1967: 45–6).

What has Tillich left for the world of learning?

This question is asked in summary form not because it will lead to an examination of Tillich's philosophical or theological legacy. That is for others far more competent to assess. What, however, does he tell us that is worth holding on to at the end of the century as a defence of the university as a foremost institution of Western civilization? It may be that Tillich's major contribution is not to be found in any grand scheme of defence nor in a proposal for reconstruction, but in a demonstration of the enjoyment of learning and teaching throughout his life's work. Indeed, he himself would wish for no better legacy for an existentialist thinker. The key aspects of his success as teacher and thinker are therefore apparent in his insights into the scholar's task.

First and foremost he is important in demonstrating that the scholar is not engaged in dealing with certainties. 'Ambiguity' might well be the key word of his thinking. The ambiguities of the German scholar's existence in the period overlapping the end of the nineteenth century and up to the Second World War made a doctrine of progressive certainty untenable, except to the time-servers and those who withdrew from any public arena. The post-1945 rebuilding period was no better for the thoughtful senior academic wishing to justify learning as an activity of reassurance. Tillich, like others of his persuasion, was sceptical about the universities being used politically as agents of public consolation or therapy.

Second, and perhaps as important in terms of internal morale, is Tillich's passionate advocacy of the excitement of learning. Who would now risk a phrase like 'ecstatic reason'? We have suffered the effects of years of dubious advocacy of experiential methods and of subliminal or psychodelic experience. What we must not neglect, however, despite the experiences of these false pathways, is the conviction that the act of learning as an excitement and an adventure of intellect is not yet dead. Plainly, much academic research is a long way from a persistent thrilling high pitch of scholarly fever. The term 'donkey work' is readily applicable to much of the effort needed to produce good research and good teaching. What Tillich reminds us is the in-built possibility that the spark is always ready to be ignited as the search is resolutely pursued. So much of the literature about the university of the end of this century is about earnest endeavour. In the puritan language of commercial management, the business of learning is reduced to inputs and outputs, to performance indicators and to consumer satisfaction. The universities themselves are forced into these modes of language as they adopt defensive postures. Perhaps both the worlds, business and academic, need reminding that people can engage in learning and also in public action with zest and enjoyment.

References

Lyons, J. (Ed.) (1969). *The Intellectual Legacy of Paul Tillich*. Detroit, Wayne State University Press (Appendix, letter from Paul Tillich to Thomas Mann).
Martin, B. (1963). *The Existentialist Theology of Paul Tillich*. New Haven, Conn., College and University Press.
May, R. (1974). *Paulus: A Personal Portrait of Paul Tillich*. London, Collins.
Pauck, W. and Pauck, M. (1977). *Paul Tillich: His Life and Thought*. London, Collins.
Sartre, J. (1984). *War Diaries*. Translated by Q. Hoare. London, Verso.
Tillich, P. (1936). *The Interpretation of History*, Part 1. New York, Charles Scribner.
Tillich, P. (1962). *The Shaking of the Foundations*. Harmondsworth, Penguin.
Tillich, P. (1964). *Theology of Culture*. New York, Galaxy.
Tillich, P. (1967). *My Search for Absolutes*. New York, Touchstone Books/Simon and Schuster.
Tillich, P. (1968). *Systematic Theology*. Welwyn, Herts, J. Nisbet.

8

Miguel de Unamuno: 'University, Unity, Universality'

The thinker represented in this chapter is in many ways the quintessentially beleaguered intellectual of the middle of this century. He spent years in exile from his university post after a brilliant early career. He was reinstated as Rector of the University of Salamanca, only to face a second, final rejection, as Spain entered the dark age of civil war and totalitarian interference with the University. In terms of wider academic reputation, he has also suffered. Unamuno might well be thought to have earned good standing with the left for his final renunciation of Franco's regime, but history has viewed his enthusiasms with suspicion, unsure where he stood in the waves of political reaction that beat on the Spanish shores in the 1920s and 1930s. He is essentially an enigmatic figure to those who came after him. His literary style, circuitous and more at home in novels and poetry than in learned articles, adds to the perplexity of his critics. Marias (1966: 5) says of him:

> His thought does not stay quiet, on the contrary, it moves incessantly from one intuition to another, but progresses by leaps conveyed this way and that by the demands of his intimate problems, his anguish and his own contradictions.

His life is that of a victim of dark forces, which, some argue, he helped to encourage by his near metaphysical enthusiasm for the spirit of the times, the soul of the nation and the idea of historical destiny. This, to many, is the language of reaction and right-wing determinism. It is not in these waters that I want to spend much time fishing; on the contrary, I believe there are more limpid and transparent streams in Unamuno's thinking about how (and why) humanity is impelled to learn, in particular at an advanced level. This chapter also reflects on what the phenomenon of the human being as a learner means in the context of the relation between the university and the state.

The key texts: The academic year opening addresses

If I have begun by concentrating on the ambiguity of Unamuno's contribution, a correction can be made instantly by emphasizing something on which he is quite clear, the value of the university in society. Unamuno produced, of course, thousands of words in his long public life as a leading member of the University of Salamanca. In common with the approach to the other writers in this volume, I have selected, from this array of polemic, a key text. It is, or rather they are, two related speeches delivered at a crucial time in the University of Salamanca's and his nation's history. The first, the most important for our theme, was an address in 1931–2 when, as rector, he opened the academic year. The second was three years later, so many inexorable steps closer to the 'Spanish Tragedy', as Koestler was to call it. The second address was delivered in 1934 at the beginning of that academic session.

The 1931 address is about unification, the unifying force of the university and the desperate need for harmony in Spain. The rector reminds his audience (composed evidently of 'secular' authorities, civic dignitaries, as well as the academic community) about his own disturbed history. He openly confesses he has delivered disruptive speeches in this same assembly, but he opines that disagreement and controversy are the very life stuff of academia. The essential fact of the university as a place for disagreement should not, however, blind us to the other truth that the institution will only survive if it rises above attempts to impose political solutions aimed at unanimity. Culture is above what he denigrates as 'the accidents' of government or, as we might put it, the temporary short-term nature of politics. In a long passage surveying the disturbed history of Spain since the Reformation, Unamuno concentrates on the momentum towards national unity and 'imperiality'. The University of Salamanca, he claims, played a leading part in the progressive drive that overrode the divisive forces in Spanish history, exerted by regionalism and by external conquerors. In what must be to many etymologists an extraordinary (but typical) play with words, Unamuno finds a significant connection between the words 'university', 'unity' and 'universality'. Like culture, the university is universal and above the expedient. He illustrates how Salamanca itself was able to bridge the regional differences of Leon, Castile and even of his native individuality: 'The spirit of universality overcomes all differences and bitterness' (Unamuno 1931: 1008).

In sombre mood, he reminds his audience of the disintegrating forces in contemporary modern Spain. One important message for the younger members of his audience at such a dangerously divisive time is that age is irrelevant in terms of value. What is new may be dead, what is from antiquity may be permanently youthful. The times ahead will test the disciplines which, as students, they will acquire in their courses. Political differences are contingent, temporary and accidental. Culture in the form of the studies pursued in a university rises above such disintegrating elements, for the university is a timeless unifier.

The 1934 address has an underlying similar theme, but this time its message is noticeably more oblique and hidden. Perhaps the times had drawn the University and its rector even closer to the fire of civil danger. Plain speaking about universities which should override temporary political masters was no longer so easy to deliver. Despite the risks, Unamuno left his audience in no doubt that he had not changed. In this message to the University, he reinforced his view of its superiority over political immediacy.

In a fascinating oblique start to the 1934 address, Unamuno suggests that in many ways there is a true popular 'University of Spain', namely the café and the public square. He moves on then to the permanent value of the oral tradition in Spanish culture, and the pure value of the spoken word. Much of the disquisition is an elegant musing on the discipline of the 'history of the tongue'. The purpose of the account suddenly becomes apparent when he relates the value of the study of the mother tongue to the hidden unity that this linguistic study reveals: 'To co-exist is to tolerate one another, and to tolerate is to understand one another.' The language of a country, even in its diverse dialectal forms, is a unifying force. 'Dialect' and 'dialectical' are, to this speaker, closely related in meaning as well as in derivation. Every paragraph after this turning point in the lecture emphasizes the importance of integration over and against disintegration, of unity against disunity, of truth and honesty against party politics. A key quotation illustrates how again he sees the university as a major factor in the nation. He says of himself that he is the university man of universal Spain ('hombre universitario de la Espana universal': Unamuno 1934: 1087). He ends with what our hindsight can see clearly as a pathetic last-ditch appeal to the students to save Spain and their elders from the madness of civil conflict.

Both these passages, in some ways workaday examples of the rituals in which leaders of universities, colleges and schools frequently must indulge, raise the debate about the university's mission to a new level of seriousness. We should expect no less from a thinker with such wide-ranging concerns for the human condition. Although I shall return to the relationship he proposed between university and state, I want now to examine in more accessible and more famous works how Unamuno was able to view the purpose of higher education as one of elevated responsibility. Three works, famous in their time, provide a consistent theme: *Tragic Sense of Life* written in 1913, *The Agony of Christianity* written in 1931, and a study of Don Quixote in 1905. The origin of all these works lay in his deeply pondered and, it might be considered, his overriding concern for the essentially tragic condition of human existence. That near obsessive preoccupation was the basis for his theory of epistemology. It explains his comprehension of how humanity is driven, even haunted by the need to learn and to study.

The human condition: The springs of intellectual activity

A good starting point is to examine Unamuno's explanation of how and why human beings engage in thought. Two initial points must be made before we can examine this theory of knowledge or, more simply, before we answer the question why we occupy ourselves with intellectual activity instead of other activities. The first is that he begins and ends in the human psyche. It is what the individual learns from social interaction that, in the end, provides the basis for his highly individualistic explanation of reason, or, as he sometimes calls it, 'reflective knowledge'. The second and, in many ways, the main message, is that the nature of our tragic condition is that both reason and experience confirm that death limits all of us, but will and feelings impel us to life and to a hope of immortality. We live, therefore, in conflict.

This essentially contradictory and apparently defeated condition of humanity is the very source of its achievement and, in the context we are considering, the origin of thinking and of intellectual activity. Unamuno is hardly unique in locating the origin of academic study and of all other intellectual activity in curiosity, but he attempts a more elaborate explanation of its derivation than is usual. His thesis is that knowing initially arises from the necessity and the will to survive. It is a faculty common to men and animals, but, in humanity, there is an additional drive. Unamuno seems to suggest a desire to know, which in its turn becomes a new kind of necessity. This extra will to know is the origin of what he calls 'reflective knowledge'. This more complex level of knowledge which reflects upon what it has discovered is the engine of intellectual activity.

So far this theory rests on little more than an individual's drive to defeat extinction. In order to elaborate, he calls upon the social context in which the individual lives. Society, he says, owes its being and its maintenance to the collection of individual drives in order to perpetuate the species. These drives are both individual and social, for the individual attempts to perpetuate himself or herself by offspring, and society desires as well as encourages the continuity of the group. The 'social instinct', he claims, is love in its most rudimentary, physiological form.

At this point Unamuno is suggesting that two kinds of reality are created by the human power to think. The first is a reality of the senses required by the individual to stay alive in a hostile environment; the second is a reality arising from social life together. There is no doubt that Unamuno regards the emergence of this second human facility as a superior tool. At one point he equates it with imagination. As we shall see, it is a widely branching form of activity, since it occupies a person's emotions and will as well as the mind: 'There is a world, the sensible world, that is the child of hunger, and there is another world, the ideal world, that is the child of love' (Unamuno 1954: 26).

Unamuno attempts an explanation of how thinking, which originates as we have seen in the necessity to survive, is converted into a more complex faculty of reason or 'reflex and reflective knowledge'. Because we exist in society, we communicate and language is born. As a result of talking to others, 'we talk with ourselves', which is to think because thought is inward language. Unamuno's philosophy is about the development of the individual mind, but it is at root a philosophy of human beings in society.

Philosophy, the whole person and all humanity

At the end of the second chapter of *Tragic Sense of Life*, Unamuno applies this theory to the question of why we philosophize? In the process of answering the question, he illustrates the essential features of his own use of thought. Again, he begins with the individual, but not only with his or her mind, but the whole person. Philosophy is a product of the heart and of the head. We philosophize for some end: 'In fact he philosophises in order to live.' There are many false ends such as consolation or distraction, but the ultimate questions for the philosopher are:

> Whence do I come and whence comes the world in which and by which I live? Whither do I go and whither goes everything that environs me? What does it all mean? The drive to philosophise, its energy and its starting point is our desire to persist indefinitely. (Unamuno 1954: 32)

This drive and desire is, again, what each one shares with others. The will to persist is social and the philosopher therefore raises these essential questions not for himself alone but for all humanity.

I have taken some time to untangle the line of argument, not to demonstrate logical consistency (for Unamuno is hardly that kind of writer), but to introduce three essential points, the view that intellectual life is concerned with 'the whole person', that Unamuno attempts an argument for the creative power of social dialogue and a form of dialectic and, above all, that he sees that out of the tragic sense of life emerges a positive, hopeful engagement.

It is immediately apparent even from the above brief references to his work, that Unamuno posits a form of knowledge distinctly different in purpose and in method from the understanding of knowledge commonly aired in educational discussions. Some of its features need to be enunciated. Its purpose is not to serve itself: 'Knowledge for the sake of knowledge, truth for truth's sake, this is inhuman' (Unamuno 1954: 29). Reason is not the sole method of enlarging knowledge. Quotation after quotation confirms his view that we know with all elements of our being: 'For the merely and exclusively rational man is an aberration and nothing but an aberration' (Unamuno 1954: 101).

It is important to note that Unamuno does not simply reject reason, but he believes that reason alone is insufficient. Because he believes in other ways of knowing, he places weight on communication through a different mode, e.g. his own writings, poems and plays. Unamuno does not separate and rank in a hierarchy different kinds of knowledge. On the contrary, he talks about the ways of knowing which are available to all kinds of thinker.

To ask a typical Unamuno question at this point, 'To what end is this engagement in a life of thought?' It is not, as we have seen, merely to satisfy curiosity, nor is it for 'therapy'. The 'authentic thinker', fully rounded, achieves a static peace. He is still part of the unalterable agony of existence in that his philosophy will not shield, cure or absolve him from dying. Indeed, the very engagement in the act of authentic knowing may initially awaken the thinker to despair. Whereas others may sleep in ignorance, the intellectual may be dangerously awake, for 'consciousness is a disease'. It is because of Unamuno's concentration on the depths of despair and the apparent still centre of agony that he speaks to us today. His message is worth listening to because, ultimately, it is about intellectual energy, the energy to continue rather than about the gloom that disables. It may be more important to seize this message for the future health of the university than to spend time on the pursuit of some politically secure role for the institution. The university in short is the arena of agony, not because it is in a temporary state of disequilibrium with the state, but because that arena is its natural, appropriate context.

Learning and the role of dialogue

The previous point is not unfamiliar to readers of existentialism or, indeed, to those who study the drama or poetry of the 1930s. Out of the depth from time to time a message of redemption was uttered. It is important to note that from the depths Unamuno is also offering hope. The sources of his hope are in the tensions between human possibility and human limitation. Another dialectical aspect of his thinking (and it is at the heart of his attitudes to learning) is his belief that human relationships can help to develop fully the power of human thought. The two significant figures in Unamuno's pantheon are Don Quixote and Sancho Panza, around whom at least one of his major works is concentrated. Panza is at one and the same time a rational realist and a man of irrational faith. He is a rationalist who, in his faithful loyalty to Quixote, learns to cast doubt on his own reason. Quixote, on the other hand, is at heart a man of despair, but an 'heroical despair' whose soul 'was the battle-ground of reason and immortal desire' (Unamuno 1954: 120). These differences and contradictions, both within the two characters and betrween the two characters, when put into action create a new form of imagination which has immense consequences for modern civilization. Unamuno has a broad sweep: 'It is not I myself alone, it is the whole human race that is involved' (Unamuno 1954: 123).

The interaction of Quixote and his servant may be grounded in despair or failure, but their engagement together is still a form of human triumph. Instead of a form of life offering sameness, unity and identification, we have presented to us here a proposal for pursuing contradictions, oppositions, tensions and, in short, living with risk and agony. This complex scene is the connection with the world of learning in school or in university. Unamuno claims that the very difficulties of living are the root of man's desire to learn. In a significant passage he says that 'Man's highest pleasure consists in acquiring and intensifying consciousness, not the pleasure of knowing exactly but rather that of learning' (Unamuno 1954: 229).

If a university ever required a motto, I would suggest 'not the pleasure of knowing exactly but rather that of learning exactly' to be nailed above the ceremonial entrance. This fundamental distinction between knowing and learning in academic life has been neglected. The old distinction between education and training, so often attempted in educational disquisitions, could be clarified with attention to learning rather than to knowing. Learning, as an activity of the teacher as well as of the taught, is easily assumed when we discuss research as an activity, but it is too easy to assume that universities have two classes, those who learn and those who have completed learning. The term 'graduate' has in this sense a fatal flaw of completion or the end of learning, which most academics know to be an untruth. Unamuno offers a challenge to all levels of academic endeavour. What is rarely admitted, at least in stiffer Anglo-Saxon academic cultures, is the possibility of pleasure and the intensifying of consciousness which is the gift made possible to senior academics as well as to juniors.

The university as an organization of conflict, contradiction and the tragic sense

If Unamuno's social psychology, his sense of the interaction between people, is centrally important and presented to us in many literary modes, we find he offers in his major published work little or no direct writing about institutions. Like many existentialist writers, he is long on social interaction and short on social structures. It is not, however, difficult to import his discussion of inherent conflict and contradiction into a specification of the nature of the ideal academic institutions. In the nearest thing to institutional study, his *Agony of Christianity* (Unamuno 1974), Unamuno sees that when men are engaged together they are engaged in struggle. The 'agony' in the title of the work is the original Greek sense of *agon*. On the plane of individual psychology. Unamuno considered, as we have seen, that there was a permanent struggle between life (maintaining hopes for immortality) and truth or reality (which kills these hopes). On the institutional plane, he sees this same struggle acted out as a great drama. This view is alien to those whose quest for continuous reposeful morale is disturbed by the idea of conflict; so, for those who put tradition first at the expense of differences, Unamuno's persistent themes of argument and variety are seen as disruptive and deviant. To Unamuno the basic life forces that dominate the world of the institution cannot be avoided or hidden away. The scholar must engage in the struggle between these elementary forces. Furthermore, the scholar should do so with zest. Indeed, one of the graces of this writer, agonized as he is and always returning to his tragic theme, is the commitment to learning as a form of joy:

> And if thereby I can confirm and sustain the same desire in someone else, perhaps when it was dwindling in him, then I shall have done a human's work and, above all, I shall have lived. (Barea 1952: 35)

I find a similar echo in an earlier source. This is Mark Pattison on intellectual endeavour, quoted by John Sparrow, which could well have been a statement from Unamuno at his most assertive about the endeavour of learning (although here the word 'knowledge' is used in a different way than Unamuno uses it):

> If ever you have realised its existence lay hold of it, never let it go – the life of the soul will give you joy beyond all other joys . . . the true slavery is that of the doers to that free idle philosopher who lives not to do or enjoy, but to know. (Sparrow 1967: 131)

The university's political function

To sustain morale might be considered by some as a highly respectable and sufficient function in any political scale of values for any institution serving the society. It is not difficult to imagine, from some of the literature in public circulation, that education as a whole should be seen as a form of morale boost or a therapy for a divided society, a consolation for public disarray. Such a solution, we have seen, is not acceptable to other writers in this volume. To Unamuno it would have been anathema. Consolation is not the function of the philosopher, nor of the institution he or she serves. Equally, other well-tried and apparently obvious justifications for the social role of the university are not within Unamuno's mission statement. The problem with 'commonsense' justifications for the pursuit of knowledge is that they appear to be rational and, for this writer, the rational is a complex area of attention.

One of the reasons I have placed this writer in this volume after other, younger thinkers about the nature of learning, is that he essentially illustrates what some have called an 'anti-rational' line of argument. As the example of this attitude, he will usefully reinforce and I hope cause reflection on my argument in the introduction to this book that there is room for different voices to be heard and a variety of ways of contributing to the late twentieth-century discussion of the role of higher education. At this stage, however, I shall concentrate on the immediate context of Unamuno's method of determining the public purpose of the university. That definition rested on a deep-seated distrust of solutions based upon narrow forms of reasoning. In Unamuno's own time as in our own, opposed positions united on an assumed common ground of agreement, for instance on the view that the university is a Palace of Reason where rationality can be applied for the benefit of the state. Following this argument, a university's scientific achievement, being both the peak of rationality and concurrently an obvious public benefactor, is taken to be the core subject of university activity. Science or technology may be thought to be the dominant area of study, taking precedence over other activities which are irrational and therefore of the past. An apparently opposing view, that the university exists to be the thorn in the flesh of society rather than its benefactor, is on close examination often equally based on rationality. Rational analysis is to be applied as an acid test to public folly and, above all, to what at first sight appears not to be folly. The uneducated, errant, non-rational world of public affairs will, in this view, succumb to the Greater Mind of the university. Unamuno would not take either of these two simple positions, at least in such stark terms. Reason, and the institutions such as the law and the universities where reason is encouraged as an essential activity, is one major human device which creates civilized society. It is, however, not the only gift at humanity's command. Its fruits should be checked to see if they are wholesome or lead to inhuman solutions. The university which leads by unchecked rationality 'educates' its students so that they despair or become slaves of an imposed system, thereby losing their freedom, rationalized out of their liberty. That is not the ideal place of learning. Therefore, the task of the teacher in a university is to temper the rational with other dimensions and he or she can find these extra dimensions of understanding life from an unusual source, from common humanity.

In an early essay of 1898 examined by Barea (see Barea 1952) entitled 'Life is a dream', Unamuno tackled the public duty of the university philosopher in an actual political situation. The occasion was the defeat of Spain in the Cuban War. That situation, he argued, if tackled in purely intellectual terms, would deal with anxiety about fame, national honour and eventually lead by reason and logic to certainty of national failure and death. He contrasted the alternative provided by the non-intellectual, uneducated poor. Their traditionalist, religious beliefs sustained them with hope – they were 'safe in dreams'. This early disquisition illustrates both the importance he attaches to the mind of common humanity as a balance against what he saw as the escalating despair of a purely rational education, and his reliance on faith or, perhaps to be more accurate, on the pursuit and quest of faith.

It is important not to be left with a simple view of Unamuno, the arch-Romantic, the admirer of poverty, faith and ignorance as opposed to educated despair. In fact, as Barea illustrates in his excellent brief introduction to the writer, Unamuno moved in his major works to the view that nobility and true human achievement were accomplished only after a pilgrimage starting with an open-eyed rational understanding that the human condition is initially conceivable as desperate. Education which offered a false consolation masking reality was dangerous. In *The Agony of Christianity*, for instance, he castigates the Jesuit educators for their attempt to deliver Christianity from life's essential, unavoidable agony: 'They administer the fatal opium of their spiritual exercises and their education' (Unamuno 1974: 87). The true educator, on the contrary, sees the contradictions of life – hoped-for certainty against the unlimited unknown nature of death, the agony of wanting immortality and the clarity of knowing it cannot be – and yet makes that vision a new source of imagination. The transcendence of the tragic is 'the very foundation of the common sharing of humanity'. Probably one of Unamuno's major claims to be an inspiration to teachers is that he can show them a noble task. He puts before them a responsibility to draw their students to see the dual version of the world, and thereby they and their students make a gesture of universal solidarity with all human endeavour: 'It is not I myself alone it is the whole human race that is involved, it is the ultimate finality of all' (Unamuno 1974: 123).

It is significant that this overwhelming plea for universality in *Tragic Sense of Life* is preceded by a specifically Spanish literary analysis, again a study of Don Quixote. Unamuno proceeds through the medium of literary analogy to a philosophical statement, a typical passageway of thought. From metaphor, through analogical language, he is able to propose that the university has a gift to offer. Again, he does not dismiss reason. We do him an injustice by using the term 'anti-rational', for we are over-simplifying and polarizing what he said. He accepts reason as one of the points of tension which makes for a new creative synthesis. Quixote is 'the battleground of reason and immortal desire' (Unamuno 1974: 120). The university, as he emphasized in both the preliminary speeches with which we started this chapter, is a place which encourages and sustains unity but does not dissolve contradictions. In this holding together of what would rationally be opposites, it is able to offer to humanity a hope, where logic would inexorably offer despair.

The university as a dialogue of contradiction

There is a clear indication in various sources that Unamuno would find common ground with other writers in this collection. Like them, if he had to talk about 'method', he would propose the dialectical method as most appropriate to the ideal university. The process is not Socratic in the sense of pursuing and hunting down truth. Encounter itself is the quarry. Valdes and Valdes (1973) have carried out research into a vast array of Unamuno's minor works, notebooks and notes on reading, for his range of reading was very wide. Consistently with the major works, they found continuous emphasis not on the lonely scholar but on the meeting of different minds. Even the discovery of the searcher's own individuality through this process is not an isolated task setting the scholar apart from others, for 'it is not the learning of facts or definitions, but rather the knowledge acquired´ by an intellectual encounter through communication' (Valdes and Valdes 1973: xxx). Unlike Marxist dialectic, however, the point of the exchange between people is:

> not a synthesis or compromise agreement of two points of view, it is exclusively the self-discovery brought about by opposition through a verbalisation or search for verbalisation of personal insights. (Valdes and Valdes 1973: xxxi)

The university, the liberal free university unshackled from political bondage, is the arena in which 'verbalization' takes place. Again we return to Unamuno's insistence on the importance of the word. More than any other defining criterion, it could be said that the university is the place of language. It is in one of its forms a Tower of Babel which has succeeded because it is the place where participants create unity while they contribute, but do not lose their individuality. This ideal type of university, with an emphasis on loquacity, is the inevitable enemy of the crudely unifying totalitarian state which drives out variations of expression and manages in a unidimensional manner. A talkative opposition is likely to lead to political suppression. The burning of books by the oppressor is the physical demonstration of anger at the multitude of voices within their covers.

In two ways, then, Unamuno's ideal university opposes the state which has its roots in crude rationalism. First, the university provokes the state to reveal the essential irrationality of its behaviour by its acts of suppression of differences and, second, the university ridicules the rational society's apparent confidence in the power of reason to eradicate the dark side of life from the human condition. We return again to the limitations set by human mortality. Unamuno's philosophical debt to Kierkegaard is very apparent at this juncture of our explication. Paradoxically, death cannot be comprehended unless life is lived fully. Reason alone will not lead anyone to solve the question of death, but the philosopher who has experience of a full life lived in dialogue with others can surmount the limitations of being human. Such a teacher should strictly be called the 'philosopher/artist'.

In the essay 'Nicodemus the Pharisee', included in the collection with the *Agony of Christianity*, Unamuno specifically dwells on the 'ills of our educational system'. Nicodemus is only capable of offering his intelligence 'aggravated by intellectualism', whereas Jesus Christ answers Nicodemus's question like a child. It is at moments like this, in an essay or more commonly in his novels, that Unamuno resembles most closely the oblique critical view of a writer like Dostoevsky. In an interesting essay comparing the two writers (Barber and McGrath 1982), Weinstein applies to both of them the term, 'The Anti-Modern Personality'. With such a pithy slogan or summary of Unamuno's message, we can see the seed of the opposition that he created for himself. Perhaps we also appreciate the explanation of why his writing carries little political weight today. He is a writer who does not use the language of progress through rationalism, and therefore is not admitted to the circle of contemporary discourse. I believe that Unamuno, if he were alive today, would argue that those who exclude the vision of the philosopher/artist condemn themselves ultimately to a dialogue of false hope and a circular discussion of despair. Standing clear, in opposition to that view, Unamuno is the essential philosopher of hope, despite the unlikely, dark starting point of his argument. To quote one of his most important disciples: 'A thinker who teaches how to turn conflict, contradiction and despair into a source of strength has something to give to men of this age' (Barea 1952: 58).

One final judgement about Unamuno's contribution is inevitably an idealistic one. Unamuno's is, in many ways, the most ambitious of the schemes for a university's public role. Just as, in his first address, he argues that the University of Salamanca will unify the region of Spain in which it is situated, so he sees the University's studies encouraging the spirit of political unity across Spain. Do we learn political lessons from our experience of university life or do we and our students pass through the experience with only one part of our being, at least our intellect, changed and developed? The answer to this question must depend upon the individual experience, but here we are discussing the 'idea'. One further disclaimer: we are not discussing day-to-day forms of university government. The question Unamuno raises is, 'Could universities and colleges act as exemplars, as models of an ideal republic, held up against the actual republic of the state?' In asking this question, we are raising again the issue of 'formal cause': for what purpose does the university exist? Unamuno's answer is a deeply serious response to the search for the good society or the idea of a *Res Publica*.

The term 'republic' in the last paragraph is taken from William Wordsworth's reflections of 1805, from the ninth book of his autobiographical poem *The Prelude*. He muses on the influences that disposed him 16 years previously in his youth to welcome the French Revolution. Subservience to God and nature, the 'fellowship of venerable books' and the freedom of spirit found in the mountains played a vital part, but alongside his own experiences of egalitarian communities. The first such experience was in the Lake District's ancient social structures. The second is a surprising source of democratic inspiration, if one remembers the third book of *The Prelude* and its measured criticism of the then unreformed Cambridge of the 1780s. In book IX, Wordsworth presents us with a lofty idea of a university, which would be difficult to present today to a common room or senate without fear of cynicism and outright rejection – and yet . . . In the lines that follow, we have an ideal presented which justifies the term 'university', a sense of inclusion, of the potential for a variety of ways of thinking 'upon equal ground':

> . . . Nor was it least
> Of many debts which afterwards I owed
> To Cambridge and an academic life
> That something there was holden up to view
> Of a republic, where all stood thus far
> Upon equal ground, that they were brothers all
> In honour; as of one community –
> Scholars and gentlemen – where, furthermore,
> Distinction lay open to all that came,
> And wealth and titles were of less esteem
> Than talents and successful industry.
> (Wordsworth 1979: 323–32)

Put aside for a moment the practical matters, such as grades of professor, of ranks of graduate and postgraduate, which appear to deny Wordsworth's 'equal ground'. Forget temporarily at least the social class composition of faculty and student group. 'Scholars and gentlemen', 'wealth and titles were of less esteem' (today, an exclamation mark seems essential). It is, however, possible in considering an ideal university or college to believe that 'distinction' lies 'open to all'. We must surely add 'It ought to be so'. If it can, then what effect might this openness have on students? The three or four years of student life for most students is a relatively small proportion of their adult life, yet it is patently a powerful period of influence. I believe it is possible to see that seminal influence affecting the political nature of the communities into which the student graduates. Obviously, this is a huge responsibility to put upon a university's shoulders. Let us temper the problem by saying that the university cannot be assumed to take that responsibility alone. It is one among many agencies that prepare the democrat. Nevertheless, we ought to ask of our institutions, do they present an experience that Unamuno paints here so ambitiously? Is this idea of a democratic influence quite dead?

I shall now turn in the concluding chapter to consider the tradition and the legacy of these writers and make some further personal comments on their significance.

References

Barber, B. R. and McGrath, M. J. G. (Ed.) (1982). *The Artist and Political Vision*. West Brunswick, Transaction Books.

Barea, A. (1952). *Unamuno*. Cambridge, Bowes and Bowes.

Marias, J. (1966). *Miguel de Unamuno* (translated by F. M. Lopez-Morillas). Cambridge, Mass., Harvard University Press.

Sparrow, J. (1967). *Mark Pattison and the Idea of a University*. Cambridge, Cambridge University Press.

Unamuno, M. de (1931 and 1934). *Obras Completas*. Madrid.

Unamuno, M. de (1954). *Tragic Sense of Life* (translated by J. C. Finch). New York, Dover.

Unamuno, M. de (1974). *The Agony of Christianity* (translated by A. Kerrigan). London, Routledge and Kegan Paul.

Valdes, M. J. and Valdes, M. E. (1973). *A Unamuno Source Book*. Toronto, University of Toronto Press.

Wordsworth, W. (1979). *The Prelude, 1799, 1805, 1850* (edited by J. Wordsworth, M. H. Abrams and S. Gill). New York, W. W. Norton.

9

Conclusion: Inheritance and Legacy

One of the themes of this book has been that the variety of debate about higher education is a virtue not a vice. Alasdair MacIntyre expresses this well:

> So when an institution – a university, say, or a farm or a hospital – is the bearer of a tradition of practice or practices, its common life will be partly, but in a centrally important way, constituted by a continuous argument as to what a university is and ought to be or what good farming is or what good medicine is. Traditions, where vital, embody continuities of conflict. Indeed when a tradition becomes Burkean, it is always dying or dead. (MacIntyre 1981: 206).

The writers in this volume, it has been emphasized, have different proposals to make, but often an undefined but observable unity of approach. It is a belief in a meeting place for differences. They belong to a tradition which is high-lighted when Newman's text is taken as a starting point. One of the difficulties of this kind of survey of ideas is that it is easy to fall into the simplistic view that each 'great name' is an inventor of an idea or that a primitive idea is redeveloped by a mind of a genius. Although I would not wish to demur from the view that some of these writers were highly gifted and original thinkers, I am sure that it is more productive to consider each thinker as an inheritor of ideas and as some-one who passes on a legacy. This conclusion, then, will briefly consider the West European tradition of thinking about the university and then move to indicate what happened to the ideas this tradition left to us.

The tradition

The radiance of Newman is so powerful that it is easy to imagine that his idea of a university sprang newly-minted from the challenge of founding a Catholic university in Dublin. We have already seen in Chapter 2 that Newman owed much of his theory to the experience of an Oxford college. I now want to make a different point about the context in which Newman operated. It is also a point relevant to the twentieth-century writers in this volume. The problem of the universities (or, as it is frequently called 100 years later, 'the crisis') was as much debated in the first half of the nineteenth century as it has been for most of the twentieth. The major changes to the almost moribund Western European universities at the close of the period culminating in the Enlightenment and, in France, in revolution, were occasioned by some familiar developments. One was the rapid development of 'knowledge' and the sub-division of areas of study, for example fuelled by the growth of public speculation about natural history. The second was the spirit of seriousness which paralleled the questioning of the purposes of ancient institutions which had previously been taken for granted. Demographic issues cannot be ignored either. The new generation of leisured classes, fed by the success of the first generation of industrialists, meant a revival of interest in a period of learning as a process of personal as well as professional education. In England, the influence of a moral earnestness in the universities undoubtedly meant that some parents found Oxford and Cambridge marginally safer places for young men to attend than they had been in the mid-eighteenth century.

The name that is usually identified with the renewal of the Western European university is William von Humboldt (1767–1835), the founder of the University of Berlin. There has been a tendency to polarize the German professional system and the Oxford or Cambridge college tutorial system and to put Humboldt's name firmly at one end of the spectrum and Newman's at the other. In doing this, we are perhaps at the mercy of the way that nineteenth-century antagonists in the English system argued their divergent cases. It is also often argued that Humboldt's Berlin, in contrast to Newman's Oxford, produced a research-oriented university, with a low level of interest in teaching and a strong emphasis on science and technology aimed at producing skilled technicians for the state apparatus. As Mommsen has clearly demonstrated, research was certainly a main aim in the University of Berlin, but Humboldt believed that academic instruction and research should go hand in hand within the same institutions (Clark 1987: 60–92). Despite state pressure to produce banks of civil servants, Humboldt promulgated a central principle of academic freedom in teaching and research. The status of the powerful professor and the 'gates' of entry to university teaching of a *Habitation*, after unpaid years as a *Privatdozent*, undoubtedly marked the German system as hierarchically rooted in powerful and separated subject discipline departments. It is important, however, to recognize that what, by the end of the century, became institutions for specialized training, had their origin in Humboldt's idea of a university with 'an idealistic philosophy and rhetoric, which emphasized that the universities were directed towards a search for the truth regardless of practical application' (W. Mommsen, in Clark 1987: 62). Humboldt and Newman left behind two ideas of the university and the path they travelled was very different, but their starting point was common. Perhaps too it should be remembered that Humboldt and Newman were taking the most courageous step an academic rooted in the value of a tradition could take: they founded new universities. That step takes a degree of confidence that the inheritance travels well.

Another early figure in the history of renewed thinking about higher education should be mentioned here, Friedrich Schiller (1759–1805). Schiller was an admirer and correspondent of Humboldt and, in his turn, was admired and praised in Western Europe. The new Republic of France accorded him the dignity of the title 'Citizen' and intellectuals in many countries, including Britain, read his social documents with almost the same enthusiasm as they greeted his historical dramas. He stood, of course, as an apostle of liberalism and political freedom, as an opponent of human repression, and for the release of the human spirit. In a series of letters to a patron, eventually published as *On the Aesthetic Education of Man* (Schiller 1967), Schiller sets out a programme of education based on a study of beauty. Although he founded no university, and his ideas, though influential, were indirect in finding an institutional setting in which to flourish, he had considerable influence on those who did form universities and on other areas of intellectual life. A brief summary of his ideas reads like a list of the objectives of the writers in this volume.

Like all the writers here, Schiller was opposed to the notion of dividing and separating humanity into discrete faculties or abilities. Wholeness was vital. The sciences and the class system of the eighteenth century had caused a severance in 'the inner unity of human nature'. The purpose of education was to unite the severed parts. The letters steadily review the tension that divide men. One severance was between the intuitive and the speculative:

> While in the one a riotous imagination ravages the hard-won fruits of the intellect, in another the spirit of abstraction stifles the fire at which the heart should have warmed itself and the imagination been kindled. (Schiller 1967: 35)

Civilization and learning had contributed to *die Trennung in dem inner Menschen* (a division within man). The instrument which can reconcile this tension is fine art.

In the tenth letter, Schiller classified two forms of diversion from the true path of humanity, one route is that of the savage and the other of the barbarian. Both can be brought together by 'an education through beauty', which at the same time will 'tense and release'. The savage will have raw human nature enchained, the barbarian will have his natural humanity set free. Readers will perhaps have recognized one of the themes in this collection, namely the power of one central area of the curriculum to combine and to bring together disparate, even opposing powers.

In another letter (number 13) there is another instance of opposing powers or 'drives' in man. One presses for change, the other for changelessness. The argument here is complex and concerned with a definition of the 'person' and 'principles' of action, but the resolution is the important issue for us in our context. Culture exists to keep each of these opposing 'drives' within its proper function. By 'culture', Schiller means a study, or rather an immersion in beauty. There is, he urges, a third important 'drive', the drive of 'play'. And this drive enables man to 'play with beauty' to explore it. This activity releases and productively combines dangerous opposites:

By means of beauty sensuous man is led to form and thought; by means of beauty spiritual man is brought back to matter and restored to the world of sense. (Schiller 1967: 123)

Schiller proposed an ascending ladder of human perfection. First, there is the physical state with a passive receptiveness for the world of sense. Next is an aesthetic state to which few aspire. This level of existence frees humanity for the third and loftiest level, the moral state. This proposal is no 'art for art's sake' proposal, but a morally earnest doctrine, suggesting that Schiller's 'student' was, in the end, a changed person, affected by his education in beauty so that he could transform the world. Education has a moral purpose in the end, as it has for all the writers in this book.

Turning to specifically English nineteenth-century contexts for the idea of a university, we must remind ourselves that Newman, although in the midst of a time of turmoil about the nature of the universities of the future, was not its initiator. We have already observed Newman's own conservative involvement in reforms in Oxford and Cambridge concerning the admission of non-Church of England members. The discussion ranged far wider than this particular issue and there are a number of texts. Two, in particular, are readily available and worth reading for their relevance to a theory of education, as well as for their close parallel with some of the problems besetting the writers of the 1930s and 1940s.

The Reverend Adam Sedgwick (1785–1873), Professor of Geology in the University of Cambridge and a fellow at Trinity College, felt moved to preach a sermon on the subject of university reform in 1833. His thoughts were so important, at least for himself, that he lengthened the argument and published it in a number of editions (Sedgwick 1969). Sedgwick's sermon is a child of its time, owing much to the influence of Coleridge and Wordsworth, who, perhaps, passed on to the intellectuals like the Cambridge scientists their understanding of Kant. Take, for instance, Sedgwick's views on the subjects of the geologist's enterprise: 'The external world proves to us the being of a God in two ways; by addressing the imagination, and by informing the reason' (Sedgwick 1969: 17). Like Newman, he saw reason and imagination in partnership:

To many minds, the forms of natural knowledge presented in the abstractions of severe science, are cold and uninviting: but if we follow them with the light of other kindred studies, such as those I have endeavoured faintly to shadow out, we bring down the fire from heaven which at once gives them movement and animation. (Sedgwick 1969: 28)

Science, and in his case, geology, is therefore a fit subject for a university based on Christian principles, because it is an activity in which imagination can be active in partnership with reason. The external world is 'fitted to our imaginative powers' by a divine being. Sedgwick continues to justify the range of work in Cambridge outside the scientific spheres. Ancient languages allow us to share the product of great minds. More important, however, such studies lead us to studies of moral philosophy. It is important to remember that Sedgwick, like most of his colleagues in the university, was ordained in the Church of England. Finally, he assembles a powerful argument against a utilitarian justification of learning. In passages very similar to Newman's, Sedgwick disputes Locke's restricted views of moral judgement and quarrels with the simplistic concept of man's mind as a *tabula rasa*. Sedgwick was not alone in writing a defence of the broadly based university in which, of course, apart from his clerical duties at the cathedral in Norwich and his geological fieldwork, he spent all his working life. Contemporaries, such as Whewell, eventually master of Sedgwick's college, and Dyer, published extensive theses on the nature of a university before Newman's book was published. They all lack the illumination, if not the fire, of Newman's great work. They are defensive and conservative but have an ideal, not least the one they share with Newman and the twentieth-century writers here. This is a belief in the unity and wholeness of human nature, allied to the conviction that the university exists to serve that unity:

> We find that no parts of the visible universe are insulated from the rest; but that all are knit together by the operation of a common law. We follow this law into its remotest consequences, and we find it terminating in beauty, and harmony, and order. (Sedgwick 1969: 13)

Another very different Victorian writer on the role of the university whose work has received recent careful analysis is Mark Pattison (1813–84), of Lincoln College, Oxford. Pattison also considered the ideal university. He was immersed in a series of debates and committees about the reform of Oxford. John Sparrow has clearly brought to our attention in his study of Pattison's ideas on university education (Sparrow 1967) the adaptation he had to make in the light of his growing knowledge and admiration for the German universities, particularly Heidelberg. It is a story of a change from a passionate, conservative defence of the collegiate system, when he gave evidence to Lord John Russel's Commission in 1825, to an equally convinced and powerful argument for the power of the university which he presented to Lord Selborne's Commission of 1850. Despite this major shift of view, encouraged, as Sparrow demonstrates, by personal career disappointments in his college, Pattison still presents to us a university which has a profile not unlike the Newman idea. The emphasis is towards what was then a modernized and improved system of teaching, but the argument continues to be liberal not vocational. We have already seen, in the chapter on Unamuno, that Pattison like the best of his contemporaries and like those who followed his tradition, believed in the excitement of learning and the university's requirement to provide a context for that higher state of experience to flourish.

The legacy

Turning now from what the thinkers in this volume inherited to what influence they left behind, I shall concentrate of the area I know best, the higher education system in the UK. Where do we find evidence of the impact made, particularly by the six twentieth-century writers described here? I have made a personal point in the introduction that these writers have been excluded from debate in recent years. The evidence is, however, that in the 20 years after the Second World War, their collective ideas were directly or indirectly influential on groups of people working in higher education. I do not wish to individualize the influence of each writer and trace his particular contribution. To a small extent, I have already indicated where this might have taken place, in very different ways, particularly with Leavis, Horkheimer and Ortega. What I would like to trace briefly now is the continuing strand of attention to issues such as the need for wholeness as against growing specialization, the nature of people as learners, the importance of the university as a place where learning goes on in dialogue and, ultimately, the relation of the university to the world.

One immediate impression given by reading the British works on the nature of the university written between 1945 and 1965 is the pervading and powerful influence of Christian thinkers. This is a surprising impression. At a period when secularism was presumed to rule supreme, it is unexpected to find, at least in one intellectual tradition, an influence of some continuing power. Take, as a major example, one work which had a long-lasting effect on discussion of reforms in the era of the Robbins Report, Sir Walter Moberly's *The Crisis in the Universities*, written in 1949. This text, heavily indebted to Newman and with cross-references to Ortega y Gasset, F. R. Leavis and Karl Jaspers, was published by the Student Christian Movement and contained a liberal, Christian message. Moberly had not only been the first full-time chairman of the University Grants Committee from 1934 to 1949, but also a former head of an Oxford college and vice-chancellor of a civic university. As the historian of post-war higher education in the UK, Campbell Stewart says:

> He was in office during the war years of ghost administration and profound rethinking for a changed world, a liberal Christian, courteous, informal and scholarly and deeply involved with Oxbridge style and values, power-ful and influential with his committee, in Whitehall and with most universities. (Stewart 1989: 62)

Not only was Moberly personally influential, he left a discussion group behind, in the shape of the University Teachers' Group (eventually to form the Higher Education Group) with members who themselves played a vital part in keeping alive the discussion of values in higher education (see Reeves 1988).

An interesting chapter in the history of ideas needs to be written about the espousal of existentialism and its influence in post-war Britain. The material is readily available in studies of the arts, particularly the novel and the theatre, but less directly in public affairs, particularly in the planning of higher education. A research worker would no doubt note that it was a highly selective form of existentialism which became a favoured philosophical support for many. Jaspers and Tillich were, for the most part, readily appreciated, Tillich perhaps more favourably because of his interest in 'culture', which, since Arnold, had been the centre of the British liberal intellectual stage. The tradition found existentialism, particularly through Tillich, a welcome renewal after the trauma of the war years and 'the light that failed' from the USSR. These strands within the *Zeitgeist* came together in a marked manner at certain key points of action in public affairs enacted by certain protagonists. One such 'event' was in the evidence to the Robbins Committee.

The documents which accompany the Robbins Report, as much as the report itself, are a rich source for identifying opinions on the nature of thinking about higher education at a moment of change (Robbins 1963). Campbell Stewart says the terms of reference of the committee established in 1964 were 'comprehensive indeed', namely to review the pattern of full-time higher education within Great Britain, making recommendations for its improvement. As might be expected, the Committee became a focus for all kinds of 'pressure' and interest groups. Of interest for this study, is the considerable weight of evidence from sources such as the Church of England Board of Education and other equivalent religious groups, as well as influential individuals who wrote or spoke in the same spirit as Walter Moberly. It is more important to note what they said than how many said it. A very good example is the stout defence of the education of teachers in an environment that encouraged dialogue and the development of the mind presented by Dr Kathleen Bliss.

One particular voice can be picked out of these decades (and still continues to be a source of wisdom and provocative thought): Professor Roy Niblett, the holder of the first English chair in Higher Education, at the University of London. Niblett serves as an excellent example of the influence of the thinkers in this volume. In an article on Jaspers and Marcel, he was the first to demonstrate that the existentialists were saying things of direct importance for the development of the humanities, particularly in the newly forming universities (Niblett 1964). Major works of influence came from his pen, from general educational works such as *Education and the Modern Mind* in 1954 to specific texts on the universities and higher education through following decades. Niblett refers directly to all the writers in this book with the exception of Horkheimer. There is a similar direct line of continuity from the original inspiration of Moberly in the writings on higher education by Marjorie Reeves (1988).

One final name must be mentioned in this summary of influence. An intriguing text is Kenneth Minogue's *The Concept of a University* (1973), written when he was Reader in Political Science at the London School of Economics. Minogue's thesis is disarmingly simple. A university should not be explained in any functional sense at all. It does not justify itself on any social, cultural or public grounds. Academic activity should be carefully distinguished from intellectual activity. The latter goes on in the wider world, often as an active engagement in political life. Academics inhabit 'a secret world' with their own techniques, disciplines and visions. Minogue takes up some of the threads from the writers in the volume but rejects others. The concept of 'culture' he finds totally unsympathetic. Academic life does not exist to provide a culture which will improve the world. He baulks too at the function of other conventional ways of philosophizing about institutions. His own political science background encourages him to apply provocative linguistic analysis to such issues as the functionalism of an institution. We have to remember the circumstances in which Minogue wrote, after five years of student (and staff) disturbance. This is a defensive, withdrawing book, concentrating on 'essence', but 'essence' without potential. It is the product of years of an assault on, and abuse of, the university by all the various and warring participants that wished to use it for their own purposes. It was also written before the swing of attention of government to the nature of these 'peculiar institutions'. Minogue's argument for a 'secret world' would not stand in that flood tide longer than a slender reed, but reeds bend and recover as floods subside. This is a good note to end on before attempting a personal response to the ideas of the university presented by the seven European thinkers.

A personal conclusion: Learning as the essence

Sometimes one's own life is the best source for a theory, despite the usual risks. In many ways that is how Jaspers, Ortega, Tillich and Unamuno produced their own ideas of the university. Even Newman's painful experience of exclusion from his university undoubtedly helped to fuel the engine which drove him to appeal for a place which he wanted others to possess.

My own experiences as a student and teacher have been from the centre and the periphery. I was part of the traditional university as an undergraduate and postgraduate research student. From its outer 'suburbs' I have had opportunities to take different sightings. In the last 20 years, I have had the privilege of leading two colleges claiming their proper place in higher education and, because they were 'claiming' not 'assuming', there has been a prolonged discussion with comparable and different institutions about the nature and definition of the claim. More harrowingly, I have presided over the closing of a college. To make a balance, I have also been responsible for the birth of a new institution of higher education. To be both undertaker and midwife must have taught some lessons. I would like to set out my conditional conclusions under the headings that have consistently emerged from the writers in this volume and hope that, without necessarily repeating what has already been related, some of their influence may be perceived.

'A place reserved for understanding'

Jaspers' phrase is a good point to start this list of personal prejudices. I believe that universities and colleges are primarily concerned with a human drive to know and then to know more. In short, 'learning' not 'teaching' nor 'enquiry' nor 'frontiers of knowledge' appears to me to be the most significant activity, although teaching and research may both be concerned with learning. Everyone in the institution should be committed to learning. In terms of mission and purpose, if not in detailed function day-by-day, there can be no categorical division between those who have learned and those who are still on the way. Although common sense may suggest that some are more travelled than others, the end of the journey is never reached. To have learning at the centre of the university's mission is to make a statement about the processes of learning. I also know that 'training' and its related process, 'instruction', may usefully go on in a university, but they are minor activities and subservient to the play of the mind in learning that Western Europe pondered on as long ago as Schiller's letters. For this reason, I am convinced that, although a university may regard it as useful that students (postgraduate or undergraduate) should learn to run a business or use a word processor and so on, these activities should not dominate the student's time. They may even be taught elsewhere or in separate periods of instruction, even in another appropriate institution. The armed forces, industry and commerce have excellent training methods for practical techniques and there is nothing to stop a university borrowing them, but they are not its chief intention. For this reason, I do not agree with the apparently egalitarian view that there is an invisible continuous link between further education and higher education. The mingling of the two has not been productive in the UK. Both have different 'missions' and should pursue them separately, without false ambitions on one side and fear of being dubbed snobbish on the other. Indeed, I would go further and suggest that, if a university or college can say of a subject claiming admission to higher education, 'It could be better taught somewhere else', then it ought to go there.

To put learning at the forefront of the university's purpose is not only to say something about the definition of what is meant by being a human being, but also about the expanding possibilities of learning itself. The special nature of learning in higher education, whether it is of the sciences, the arts or the humanities, is in openness to continuous enquiry. There are few ends and many pathways leading on. The combined work of reason and imagination, which has with various terminologies occupied all the writers in these texts, still remains, in my experience, a valuable way of understanding the process of learning at this level. Hours of donkey work may be needed to achieve one moment when the whole self becomes engaged in an achievement, an instant which can only be described with a metaphor from physical sight – a moment of vision. Such moments are not as rare or as confined to 'high-fliers' in higher education as might be thought. Many students, including some who have not achieved a good class of degree, have felt something of the shock of discovery, of bringing disparate things together, in short, a time of recognition. I believe that this is particularly true during the final year of the degree course, for the process takes time. The phrase 'making sense' is used frequently of this moment, but it does not happen where the student experience has been so badly arranged that the courses make a jumble of nonsense or where there has been little or no sensibility in the teaching.

Learning requires teaching like a dance or a play requires a choreographer or a director. Choreographers or directors are helpless without dancers and actors. The mutual relationship of teacher and student, whether the work is undergraduate or postgraduate, is a vital criterion in defining the quality of higher education. The dialogue is the best part of the process of learning. I do not agree that the Socratic dialogue, so much favoured by Karl Jaspers, is the only form of learning possible. Indeed, it is singularly inappropriate for certain forms of scientific discovery, good though it may be for clarifying concepts or untangling knots of language. A university or college worth its salt must attend to what actually occurs in the teaching relationship. Frantic attempts to instruct students by machine or to encourage self-guided learning may succeed with some students, and with the acquisition of certain kinds of knowledge, but they are no substitute for a moving of minds devoted to focusing on an issue, an experiment, a poem or a problem. Of course, this manifesto is most exposed here, for the actual student experience of, say, tutorial teaching, may be very different from what we, as tutors, fondly think it is. Processes of 'evaluation', threatening though they appear, need not be feared if they are part of the basic authentic urge to know the truth, even about how we are proceeding to know the truth.

The community of learning

To be able to use this well-worn phrase is more than a gesture of hope in universities as places which informally provide and create the setting for learning to occur. We have to put against Newman's classic statement of the pervasive ambience of the residential college, two objections. The first is one I mentioned in the chapter on Newman. American and British studies of the student experience cast doubt on what the student is learning, other than what he or she would learn in any community. Similar processes of learning also occur in barrack rooms, in barristers' chambers, in industrial laboratories and in fire-station rest rooms. Much of what is learned in such places is socialization not education. The same may be true of a university's junior common room. The trouble is that we remember our own youth with easy enthusiasm and some of us correctly claim how much we learned from a residential community of a different time. Now, of course, we are catering for large numbers of students who are not part of a traditional residential community. There are older students with an experience of other walks of life, living at home with their families. What price the 'academic community' now? Indeed, for many years, too high a price has been claimed for it. Lawrence Stone (1983), in a typically provocative article, makes out a cogent argument that, in fact, the purpose of the traditional university was social control of the young. Intellectual excellence only followed the successful achievement of discipline.

Despite all these objections, I believe that the way people relate to one another, organize their time and their occupation (all contained in the dangerous word 'community') in higher education, are key aspects of the unique process called learning. We must remember that, despite demographic trends in Western Europe, our colleges and universities will still continue the traditional role of teaching young people, who use the institution as a place of 'passage' into adulthood. However, the student who is seeking a different kind of 'passage' into a further development of an adult self already achieved now must be understood as part of the 'community'. The point is that the powerful influence of the university or college can be activated by careful consideration of what is planned (or not planned) for the opportunities to meet, to work together in a common enterprise, even simply to enjoy each other's company in a place 'set apart'. I have to acknowledge Newman's vision of a *genius loci* in which learning from each other can take place, but I cannot accept his presumption that it will take place merely by the gathering together of people pursuing learning. In today's larger institutions, it is common knowledge that students from the same area of study and usually from the same year are apt to mix with each other exclusively. There is no automatic guarantee of intermingling of people from different subject disciplines. Size becomes a fact of life that the university planner has to consider and plan to override or to make use of if he or she is to establish a 'community of learning'.

Before picking up the matter of size, there is one political matter which all the seven writers share implicitly or explicitly and I share it with them: the importance of the institution. Hedge scholars may learn in or under hedges, intellectuals may operate alone or in salons, but the institutional identity of a university or college is not incidental to its purpose. It is important to recognize, underneath the changing of forms, a tradition of institutional learning which has continued at least since the late eighteenth century and, perhaps, with interruptions since medieval times in Europe. These remarks are almost so obvious as to be banal, except for one contemporary problem. As in the 1930s and 1940s, the institution itself is at risk. Universities then were closed by tyrants; now colleges and departments are eliminated by government agencies. One has to admit that there will be a moment when a college must merge with another in order to improve its intellectual standards. One can comprehend that the closure of a department may be owing to inadequate provision for learning. All these contingencies are always proposed as 'reasonable', but each one should be tested to the ultimate explanation. As long as universities or colleges and their departments are treated as instruments for the carrying out of national policy, they will be at risk of changes of policy and of values external to academic judgements. In other words, they will be close to the furnace of power, which no-one can avoid but all should view with great wariness. All the writers here would see the university as more than an instrument to affect externally driven changes. From Newman's emotional memory of the snapdragons outside Trinity College, to Unamuno's tactical appeal to the new government controlling his ancient university, these writers assume that the continuing tradition is in itself essential to the idea of the university. Institutions such as factories or shops may be treated instrumentally to purvey, display and provide goods or services. They can be replaced by others of the same type or more up-to-date versions. A college, a department or a university that closes is never replaceable in the same sense or, in many cases, never replaced in any sense. These remarks are, of course, in direct opposition to those who view human institutions with the gravest suspicion and aim to destroy them as soon as they 'degenerate' into any form of stability. Of course, all institutions of higher education have the capacity to break the individual on the massive wheel of tradition or inertia. If it were not so, there would not be so many campus novels. However, I am aligned with the writers here who would regard an assault on the continuity of ancient (and modern) institutions of higher education as an attack on freedom itself, or at least the thin end of a dangerous wedge.

The institutions of higher education have not only grown larger in themselves than their counterparts 50 years ago, there are also more institutions of different sizes and function. Some facts, taken from Campbell Stewart's summary chapter, tell the tale. Between 1951 and 1981, the number of full-time university academic staff in the UK rose from around 10,000 to about 33,000. In the 10-year period 1952–62, 14 new universities were added to the UGC list. The size of universities in the period 1938–9 to 1981–2 is also significant. In 1938–9, there were 18 universities with less than 2000 students. In 1981–2, there was one (Stewart 1989: ch. 15). These facts solely relate to universities, but add the major developments of polytechnics and colleges of higher education and there is no illusion of growth but a genuine and permanent change of setting for higher education, which is repeated in all Western European countries.

The causes are obvious. One is social, the public will that more people shall have access to higher education. In the UK, for instance, the age-participation rate for under 21-year-olds for entrance to universities in 1938–9 was 2.7% of the total 18-year-old population. For 1982–3, it was 13.5%. A significant development which has barely begun to be examined for its implication is the percentage of women students in the full-time student population in British universities. In 1938–9, it was 23.3%; in 1983–4, it rose to 39.6%. These are, to my mind, irreversible (and welcome) trends. There were also internal reasons for the development of institutions which offered more places. Particularly in science and technology, the cost of research equipment and the provision of technical services and support staff all make for larger units and concentration. The humanities are not exempt from this tendency. The growth and development of library services, linked to copyright libraries in the UK and to major libraries overseas, are expected parts of the service to research and even to undergraduate study in the non-technical subject disciplines. The fears of Ortega and Leavis, or in different respects of Horkheimer and Jaspers, about the separation of disciplines and the extinction of individuality in mass institutions look fully realized with a superificial glance at the UK. This was a country which regarded itself as being distinguished by the small institution with individual teaching and a close knowledge of students.

It is easy, however, to be overwhelmed both by facts of size and by arguments for 'critical mass' and more concentration. A large university can be organized to enable those who study diverse disciplines to meet and to share their work at all levels from undergraduate to learned work in research. The experiments at the new universities of Keele and Sussex are only two examples of deliberately constructed systems to achieve interdisciplinary objectives. This is not a complacent reassurance. Much remains to be done to make our large institutions human in scale. Experiment and failure will occur, and it is a sign of hope that new solutions continue to operate and that risks are taken in planning interdisciplinary work.

Size is not the only issue. Scale, in the sense of variety of academic activity, is also very important in determining the specific quality of the student experience. It is possible, for instance, for a small college to be so concentrated in its subject area that it rivals the worst features of a large organization in providing a narrow experience for students. I believe that most teacher-training colleges and some schools of nursing in England and Wales have been considerably improved and have justified their place in higher education by departing from their 'monotechnic' status' and diversifying their programmes. Intending teachers and nurses as well as other professionals are taught alongside students from a variety of academic disciplines and from other professions. The colleges have had to grow in size in the process, and the nature of their previously tight-knit (and sometimes inward-looking) academic communities has changed considerably. There is a danger, however, in assuming that there is one optimum size for an institution. Size is one factor in three, the others being purpose and scale of academic activity. At best, what has been produced in the UK is a varied set of institutions of higher education with the possibility of developing very different solutions to the problems of higher education. Diversity may be an administrator's headache, but it is also the elixir of fitness for a meeting of minds. It demands, of course, a degree of toleration from public administration and from political masters, which leads me to the final issues raised by these thinkers, those of the university and the public good.

The university and the state

The writers in this book present, within a reasonably unified range of views, an idea of a university which is independent from public or political direction but ultimately of great value to the state. On the subject of why the product of the university, interpreted as either the graduates or the research of the university, should benefit the public good, they are not united. Newman rested on the assurance that 'gentlemen' would rule the world and the 'cultivation of intellect' would continue to refresh the cadre of rulers that eventually governed everywhere that was red on the map. Leavis, Tillich and Ortega rely on the development of culture (or perhaps on its defence) to preserve a civilization consistently under attack. The university's function is to be the treasure-house of that culture. Ortega places an equal responsibility on the university as the only viable agency to repel the formidable tide of mass society. Horkheimer, but not he alone, interprets the institutions of higher education as centres for a critical appraisal of society. The state, in effect, should permit the existence of a place which tests public action.

It is Unamuno and Jaspers who, to my mind, give a more satisfying role for the university in our own times. They are cautious about a university being justified by social function. Like Kenneth Minogue, they argue that the academic marches to a different drummer. The effect of the university as a house of intellect is indirect. Without it, society is very much poorer – even dangerously bereft. All the writers in this volume are in no doubt that their idea of a university could create an institution which embodies civilizing forces, but it is easy to remember them only for that. They also indirectly or directly make a political point. They insist that a free university is one of the guarantees for a free society. Both Jaspers and Unamuno saw the effects of a system which did not permit 'a place reserved for understanding'. This, to me, is the principal argument for the independence of an institution of higher education: it serves to defend the independence of us all.

I do not need to labour or repeat the arguments used by each writer about the other utilitarian benefits of a university education. It should, however, be clear that the age-old battle between utilitarian and liberal is in some quarters fading a little. The industrial and commercial appeals for well-qualified people are now couched in much less specifically technical terms than a few years ago. Public statements from employers, if not yet from government, about the encouragement of open-minded creative people, regardless of the subject disciplines from which they originate, should encourage the universities and colleges to insist on what they already do well: concentration on the processes of learning. One other indirect effect of a modern higher education that universities and colleges rarely claim is exemplified by these writers. Like the students of medieval Europe, the students (by which I mean teachers, as well as undergraduates) can increasingly claim to belong to a European-wide system or at least a West European and American system. There has never been a time since the Middle Ages when movement between institutions is quite so possible. The voices in this book are, above all, European voices and, if they can act as a chorus of encouragement, they will posthumously have donated one further gift to us.

My own view is that universities and colleges can claim as fundamental a role in the public realms as health, the arts, defence and security or religious belief. Like religious belief (and for some in partnership with it), a university can fulfill the quality of life that human beings can and should claim as a right. Also, like organized religions, the university in some states is often kidnapped by politicians for their own ends, for moral reform or for the pacification of disruption. Religion and education may both reform and pacify; alternatively, they may have the opposite effects, which is presumably disturbing and disappointing to the politician. We are constantly told that the capacity for modern people to create surplus wealth and surplus leisure is unlimited, given effective organization. Higher education deserves its place in the allocation of that wealth as much as sport or art. We should not claim that higher education is the sole agent for the good life but it should be allowed its place, for on it as well as on other civilizing forces the good society depends. Arguments of justification in the philosophical field should be consistent and not diverted into economic arguments. If the message of these writers, that there is a special quality of learning related to the fulfilment of a major human potential, is accepted by those who are the learners, then the university or college must insist on the recognition of that criterion in all bids for a share of national wealth. All the rest is expediency and conditional and needs arguing in other fields than philosophy, though philosophy may be used to test those arguments.

Universities and colleges, like churches and health districts, are functionally complex institutions. Some of the functions, such as raising money to run the church, hospital or college, are directly related to the success of the enterprise. Others, such as the service to the people who inhabit the institution (e.g. sports and social activities), may be secondary but enhance the enterprise. The 'enterprise', however, rests on a single aim in all cases, despite the complexity of functions that shore it up. If this is true for churches and health districts, then it is particularly true of higher education. Every generation in the universities and colleges has to argue about that common purpose. Each decade it must be restated and redefined. The language will always be new, but I suggest that there is a long-lasting value in the essential language of these writers: to seek for truth, to extend human enquiry and to satisfy human curiosity.

Finally, one of the greatest difficulties for anyone writing personally about a long time spent in higher education is separating autobiography from other people's autobiography. It is easy to reassemble one's own youth and gild it with nostalgia in order to recreate an ideal studenthood. It is easier still to forget that a university or college means very different things to its principal, to its lab technicians, to its postgraduate doctorate student or to its fresher. When, with these writers, we talk of an 'idea', we talk of what we have glimpsed but never continuously experienced.

These writers offer doctrines of hope, a commodity in fairly short supply in European universities and colleges in recent years. For this reason alone, bearing in mind the cycles of threat, despair and hopelessness in which these twentieth-century writers struggled to carry on their teaching, we should respect the promise that they hold out to our hard-headed times. It may be that it is the language in which they express their hopes for humanity which is the major obstacle to their acceptance today. For a variety of reasons, there has been a long period of distrust of high-flown words and of rhetoric. In some, perhaps most, academic circles, 'noble ideals' are associated with the language of persuasion, with imprecision and with irrationality. Better by far, it has been said, to identify phenomena, whether social or material, precisely – even mathematically – than risk the language of enthusiasm which we have to share with the shifty worlds of advertising, politics and poetry. It has to be said again that the modern university or college is not a simple, unified entity, as it was for some of the writers in this volume. The university, for some, is an entre-preneurial institution, for others, a place for the management of knowledge; again, for one major group, it is primarily a research-oriented institution, and for many a place for teaching. Because they are multifunctional institutions, the university or college is a Tower of Babel resounding to entrepreneurial lan-guage, high-tech language, management language, as well as the diverse registers of the distinct academic disciplines. The argument of this book is not that this diversity should be reduced to a monotone. That would be impractical as well as undesirable. What we must allow within the concert of voices is a place for the language that explores why the university or college is in operation, a language of 'essences' or ideas. The other voices now appear to be dominant. They appear to be the same bodyguards of reason defending good practical sense against those who operate by flights of fancy. The group of writers in this book, from Schiller and Newman onwards, have also espoused the languages of reason. The texts examined here demonstrate that reason has its due and necessary part to play in the argument about how we learn. They do not argue that $2 + 2 = 4$, but that $3 + 1$ and $2.5 + 1.5$ reach the same conclusion. A 'republic' of learning should permit divergent pursuits of truth.

The word 'republic' is a good way to end this exploration of ideas. The university today is frequently seen in the two extreme ways that a crude political model provides. Either it is a republic within the Republic, a private city for pursuit of personal, private ends, or it is a part of the public body wholly devoted to public ends. I hope that the writers in this volume permit a play of the mind on a range of different and more responsive ideas. Personal and public in the ideal Republic can hold together. A republic inevitably continues in tension and by balancing acts. The universities and institutions of higher education deserve their own distinctive place among the varied elements in the commonwealth of Western Europe. Their traditions are maintained by giving them a place reserved 'for understanding', to use Jaspers' phrase. In return for the undoubted privilege of this position, they will enhance both the individual and the commonwealth. These are places of 'ideas' in a slightly different sense than the way that the word has been used by these writers. Unless the institutions of higher education have an idea of themselves they will not retain their honoured place.

References

Clark, B. R. (1987). *The Academic Profession: National Disciplinary and Institutional Settings.* Berkeley, Calif., University of California Press.

Jaspers, K. (1960). *The Idea of the University.* London, Peter Owen.

MacIntyre, A. (1981). *Beyond Virtue.* London, Duckworth.

Minogue, K. (1973). *The Concept of a University.* London, Weidenfeld and Nicolson.

Moberly, W. (1949). *The Crisis in the University.* London, SCM Press.

Niblett, W. R. (1954). *Education and the Modern Mind.* London, Faber and Faber.

Niblett, W. R. (1964). On existentialism and education. *British Journal of Educational Studies*, **2** (2).

Reeves, M. (1988). *The Crisis in Higher Education: Competence, Delight and the Common Good.* Milton Keynes, SRHE and Open University Press.

Robbins, Lord (Chairman) (1963). *Report of the Committee on Higher Education.* London, HMSO.

Schiller, F. (1967). *On the Aesthetic Education of Man* (edited by E. M. Wilkinson and L. A. Willoughby). Oxford, Oxford University Press.

Sedgwick, A. (1969). *A Discourse on the Studies of the University* (edited by E. Ashby and M. Anderson). Leicester, University of Leicester Press.

Sparrow, J. (1967). *Mark Pattison and the Idea of a University.* Cambridge, Cambridge University Press.

Stewart, W. A. C. (1989). *Higher Education in Post-War Britain.* London, Macmillan.

Stone, L. (1983). Social control and intellectual excellence. Oxbridge and Edinburgh 1560–1983. In *Universities, Society and the Future.* Edinburgh, Edinburgh University Press.

Index

The Society for Research into Higher Education

The Society exists both to encourage and co-ordinate research and development into all aspects of higher education, including academic, organizational and policy issues; and also to provide a forum for debate – verbal and printed.

The Society's income derives from subscriptions, book sales, conference fees, and grants. It receives no subsidies and is wholly independent. Its corporate members are institutions of higher education, research institutions and professional, industrial, and governmental bodies. Its individual members include teachers and researchers, administrators and students. Members are found in all parts of the world and the Society regards its international work as amongst its most important activities. The Society is opposed to discrimination in higher education on grounds of belief, race etc.

The Society discusses and comments on policy, organizes conferences, and encourages research. Under the imprint SRHE & OPEN UNIVERSITY PRESS, it is a specialist publisher of research, having some 40 titles in print. It also publishes *Studies in Higher Education* (three times a year) which is mainly concerned with academic issues; *Higher Education Quarterly* (formerly *Universities Quarterly*) mainly concerned with policy issues; *Abstracts* (three times a year); an *International Newsletter* (twice a year) and *SRHE News* (four times a year).

The Society's committees, study groups and branches are run by members (with help from a small secretariat at Guildford). The groups at present include a Teacher Education Study Group, a Staff Development Group, a Continuing Education Group, and a Women in Higher Education Group. The groups may have their own organization, subscriptions, or publications (e.g. the *Staff Development Newsletter*). A further Questions of Quality Group has organized a series of Anglo-American seminars in the USA and the UK.

The Society's annual conferences are held jointly; 'Access and Institutional Change' (1989, with the Polytechnic of North London). In 1990, the topic will be 'Industry and Higher Education' (with the University of Surrey). In 1991, the topic will be 'Research and Higher Education' (with the University of Leicester); in 1992 it will be 'Learning and Teaching' (with Nottingham Polytechnic). Other conferences have considered 'HE After the Election' (1987) and 'After the Reform Act' (July 1988).

The Editorial Board of the Society's imprint seeks authoritative research or study in the field. It offers competitive royalties, a highly recognizable format in both hardback and paperback and the world-wide reputation of Open University Press.

Members receive free of charge the Society's *Abstracts*, annual conference Proceedings (or *Precedings*), *SRHE News* and *International Newsletter*. They may buy SRHE & Open University Press books at discount, and *Higher Education Quarterly* on special terms.